"As a translator, and a long-time student of languages, I find the topic of mother tongues and learned languages fascinating, and the treatment it receives in these compelling essays is revelatory."

—Edith Grossman, translator of
*Living to Tell the Tale* by Gabriel García Márquez

"A rich and surprising book brimming with love of culture and respect for language."　　　　　　　　　　—*Tucson Citizen*

"This delightful collection . . . vividly recounts the process that anyone who loves words goes through: the process of falling under the spell of language's seemingly infinite potential."

—*Publishers Weekly*

"A wonderful book that is both intellectually stimulating and a great pleasure to read."

—Lara Vapnyar, author of *There are Jews in My House*

"[A] collection that should heighten anyone's awareness of the potential and the limitations of the English language."

—*San Jose Mercury News*

"A brilliant collection of writers thinking brilliantly about one of the most intimate aspects of their lives: language."

—André Aciman, author of *Out of Egypt*

WENDY LESSER

# The Genius of Language

Wendy Lesser is the founding editor of *The Threepenny Review* and the author of six books of nonfiction. Her reviews and essays appear in periodicals and newspapers around the country. She lives in Berkeley, California.

# The Genius of Language

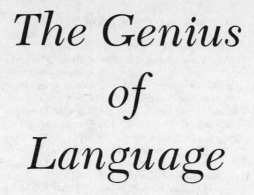

# The Genius
## of
# Language

FIFTEEN WRITERS REFLECT ON
THEIR MOTHER TONGUES

*Edited and with an introduction by*
WENDY LESSER

ANCHOR BOOKS
A Division of Random House, Inc.
New York

FIRST ANCHOR BOOKS EDITION, JULY 2005

The Library of Congress has cataloged the Pantheon edition as follows:
The genius of language: fifteen writers reflect on their mother tongues /
edited and with an introduction by Wendy Lesser.
p. cm.
1. English language—Style. 2. English language—Study and teaching—Foreign
speakers. 3. Authors, American—20th century—Biography. 4. Immigrants—United
States—Language. 5. Bilingualism—United States. 6. Second language acquisition.
7. Authors, Exiled—Language. 8. Language and languages. 9. Authorship.
I. Lesser, Wendy.
PE1421.G456 2004 820—dc22 2003060894

**Anchor ISBN: 1-4000-3323-3**

*Author photograph © Mike Minehan*
*Book design by M. Kristen Bearse*

www.anchorbooks.com

Printed in the United States of America
10 9 8 7 6 5 4 3 2

IN MEMORY OF LEONARD MICHAELS

1933–2003

# Contents

# CONTENTS

# The Genius of Language

# Introduction

## Wendy Lesser

The original idea for *The Genius of Language* was given to me by an editor, Alice van Straalen. Why not find a dozen or more writers who now write in English but who originally spoke another language, she suggested, and get them to write essays on the differences between their two languages? Normally I am against accepting ideas from editors, but this one struck me as such a good one I couldn't resist. It is an appealing notion—that there is some hidden ur-language seeping into or shaping or otherwise influencing the language in which the writer now writes. Perhaps even monolingual writers have this feeling; that may explain why one friend of mine, a poet whose sole language has always been English, heard the idea for the book and exclaimed, "Oh, I want to be in it!"

When I invited the fifteen writers included here to participate in the project, I urged them to be as autobiographical as they wished. The story of original languages, I suspected, would make itself felt not just on the linguistic or literary level, but also in the way people felt about their lives. And because those lives involved a move—often a forced move—from one country or family culture to another, these stories might well tell us something about the larger historical or political issues of our time.

But that was secondary. What mattered most to me, at the beginning, was to uncover the sources of writing in writers I admired, to burrow in behind the acquired layers and get at the inherent nature, the native quality, the "genius" of the work. Of course, what I expected and what I eventually got were not identical. Writers are like cats: you can't herd them. Life (and editing) would be far more boring if you could.

The minute you consider the category—writers who came to English after first speaking another language—the name Joseph Conrad invariably springs to mind. He is the great ancestor, the supervisory ghost, in a book like this. (Some people would add Vladimir Nabokov's name as well, but to my mind Conrad is the far greater writer: I am convinced that *Lord Jim* and *Chance* and *The Secret Agent* will be read long after *Lolita* and *Pale Fire* have bit the dust.) Since the essays in the present collection were commissioned especially for the book, I was, for obvious reasons, unable to secure a contribution from Conrad. So I am sneaking him in the back door by quoting him up front.

At the beginning of the 1919 edition of his autobiographical *A Personal Record,* Conrad takes great pains to dispel the impression that he *chose* to write in English. His first language, of course, was Polish, and his father, a well-known Polish patriot who died when Conrad was twelve, was apparently an acknowledged master of the language. Growing up in Poland, Conrad knew French, as he says, "fairly well and was familiar with it from infancy." Yet when he came to write fiction, it was the English language that seized his imagination:

The truth of the matter is that my faculty to write in English is as natural as any other aptitude with which I might have been born. I have a strange and overpowering feeling that it had always been an inherent part of myself. English for me was neither a matter of choice nor adoption. The merest idea of choice had never entered my head. And as to adoption—well, yes, there was adoption; but it was I who was adopted by the genius of the language, which directly I came out of the stammering stage made me its own so completely that its very idioms I truly believe had a direct action on my temperament and fashioned my still plastic character.

Conrad acknowledges that his relationship to the language is necessarily different from that of a native speaker. But the degree of intimacy he feels is, if anything, greater:

A matter of discovery and not of inheritance, that very interiority of the title makes the faculty still more precious, lays the possessor under a lifelong obligation to remain worthy of his great fortune . . . All I can claim after all those years of devoted practice, with the accumulated anguish of its doubts, imperfections and falterings in my heart, is the right to be believed when I say that if I had not written in English I would not have written at all.

Several of the writers collected here would and even do say the same thing about themselves. It is the crossing of a boundary, the alienation from the original tongue, which made writers of them. So a book in which various bilingual authors are asked to consider the differences between their original language and

English will inevitably be as much about the adopted language as it is about anything else. In using the phrase "the genius of the language," Conrad was referring to English, and it is that experience—the process of being embraced or enveloped by English, whether through books or movies or other people— that you will witness over and over in these pages.

Still, the intention of the book was also to stimulate some reflections on the particularities of the language of origin: that is, to get these writers to express in English the singular character- istics of their mother tongue. It is never an easy task to explain the mechanism of such literary and linguistic border-crossing (Conrad himself calls it "a task which I have just pronounced to be impossible"), but the authors I've collected here all give it a good try. Even as you read about each writer's discovery of English, you will also be learning something about the peculiar nature, the indwelling spirit, of French, or Greek, or Korean, or Russian. Sometimes the revelation will not be explicit: you will need to listen closely to pick up the tonal subtleties that inflect the adopted tongue. Sense of humor, sentence rhythm, use of adjectives, attention to time and place, penchant for anecdotal- ism or analysis, construction of the first-person narrative voice— these are all qualities that the writer may carry over from his or her original language.

I should say a few words about what this anthology is not. It is not a scholarly work in the field of linguistics or anthropology or comparative rhetoric. Nobody in this volume is a trained linguist; hardly anyone here even holds an academic post. The contributors are all writers, and they have been chosen almost entirely on the basis of their quality as writers in English, since that is the only way I could know their work. It was my assumption that we would learn something from fiction-writers and playwrights and critics and literary journalists that we would *not* learn from scholars of language.

Nor is this a representative collection, whatever that might be in a world occupied by approximately six thousand different languages. I have made some effort to get a bit of geographical distribution, but the effort is relatively weak. Huge gaps are evident: Arabic, Japanese, Portuguese (to name but a few of the major missing languages). There is only one writer from the entire African continent. There are too many former Europeans. And there are too many Jews. Part of this can be blamed on geopolitics: the vicissitudes of twentieth-century history drove large numbers of Jews into the English language, and many of them became writers. But part is no doubt the result of my limited perspective, in that my own family background is European-Jewish. You might also keep in mind that I *did* have to persuade each of the contributors to do the onerous work of writing an essay. In this context, I am reminded of the passage from Shakespeare's *Henry IV, Part One* in which Glendower claims, "I can call spirits from the vasty deep," to which Hotspur sensibly responds: "Why, so can I, or so can any man; / But will they come when you do call for them?" What you find here are the spirits that came.

The contributions do not all follow the rules—or rather, I allowed myself to break the rules in acquiring the essayists, and the individual authors went on to break more rules in writing their essays. A rigid adherence to the from-foreign-language-to-English rubric would have eliminated Ariel Dorfman (who forgot his early Spanish and had to relearn it after English) and Amy Tan (who acquired English and Chinese simultaneously) and Nicholas Papandreou (who was born in Berkeley and spoke English before Greek) and James Campbell (who never did speak Scots, though he understood the infusions of it in his mother's and grandmother's speech). An insistence on the now-they-write-only-in-English rule would have left out Josef Škvorecký (who has written books in English but continues to depend more heavily on Czech) and Ngugi wa Thiong'o (who wrote in English for many years but reverted to Gĩkũyũ for political and personal reasons) and Bert Keizer (who writes and speaks primarily in Dutch). In place of a strictly one-way journey, I have substituted a looser bilingualism which allows all my authors to comment on the relationship between English and their other languages. My notion of a "language" has been loose, too, in that I have included some that might be viewed as variants or subsets of others (Yiddish a version of German, Scots a version of English). All this latitude has produced a certain variety of approach, as has the age span of the writers, who range from their twenties to their seventies; each generation has a different story about coming to English, just as each country or culture does.

Still, there are common threads in these essays. Perhaps the most common is a tendency to equate the language of childhood with childhood itself. The tangibility of childhood experience—the tendency to join the word with the thing, so that, in Randall Jarrell's terms, "a word has the reality of a thing: a thing that can be held wrong side up, played with like a toy, thrown at someone like a toy"—is repeatedly invoked here. We have all been exiled from childhood, but because most of these writers have actually been exiled from their childhood *place*, they seem to feel that something of that lost experience still exists somewhere, accessible (if at all) only through language. You can see this most strongly, perhaps, in M. J. Fitzgerald's chapter on Italian and Gary Shteyngart's on Russian, but it is also prominently there in Bharati Mukherjee's piece on Bangla, Thomas Laqueur's essay about German, Nicholas Papandreou's discussion of Greek, and Ha-yun Jung's reflections on Korean. When Louis Begley conflates the Polish interiors of his childhood with a Polish story he once read, or when Luc Sante describes French as "my secret identity, inaccessible to my friends," we are being offered a glimpse of the writer's imaginary homeland, compounded of fiction, memory, and loss.

There is an irony to my editing a book about exile—for that is what a book about the genius of language is bound to be, just as it is also bound to be about geography, and culture, and politics, and history. Not only am I embarrassingly monolingual, possessed of the merest remnant of my little high-school Spanish and even tinier high-school Russian, but I am also the very opposite of an exile. I now live about forty miles from where I grew up, and out of my fifty years I have spent no more than six or seven away from California, the state where I was born. What all these exiled authors long for—a return to a lost place of origin, generally one from which they or their families were violently expelled—I have automatically. And yet the possession of this birthright is not so automatic that I am unconscious of it. Driving over the bridge to San Francisco, especially at dawn or twilight, I frequently look out at that familiar landscape and think of the lines from Brecht's *Caucasian Chalk Circle* about why one loves one's country: "Because the bread tastes better there, the sky is higher, the air smells better, voices sound stronger, the ground is easier to walk on. Isn't that so?" Sometimes one understands the truth of things best through absences and lacks (as Conrad grasped English more tightly because it was discovered, not inherited). It is in this way that I understand what Brecht, exiled in California when he wrote those lines, was feeling; and it is in this way that I understand what exiled writers mean when they write about their lost languages.

Another absence, too, haunts this book. Shortly before I turned in the final manuscript, in May of 2003, my dear friend Leonard Michaels died quite suddenly of complications from lymphoma. I cannot adequately convey how essential a writer he was: to me as a reader, to the magazine he helped me with for more than twenty years, and to the landscape of American literature, which he partially shaped. Perhaps his beautiful essay on Yiddish—his last major piece of prose—will begin to suggest something of what we have lost. He was a master of the precisely descriptive sentence, and his humorously apt phrases often came back to me in the course of daily life; I remember thinking, just before I learned he was ill, that I would not like to exist in a world that did not contain Lenny Michaels. Now I will have to, as will we all. It seems fitting, though hardly consoling, that a collection about the genius of language should be dedicated to his memory.

# The Way Back

## Bharati Mukherjee

There is a reason why the language we inherit at birth is called our mother tongue. It is our mother, forgiving, embracing, naming the world and all its emotions. Though I have lived for the last forty years in cities where English or French is the language of the majority, it's Bangla that exercises motherly restraint over my provisional, immigrant identity. Mother-Bangla is fixed; I haven't learned a new word nor had new thought or feeling in Bangla for nearly half a century. *I don't need to.* According to group-norms, as a native-born speaker, I have automatic membership in the world's most articulate, most imaginative and most intelligent club. With its brazen appeals to love and vanity, enforced with coercive guilt, the language sabotages irony towards the community's billowing self-esteem. Like a child whose mother might tipple or stray, I look for excuses, cannot condemn. To my inner Bengali I remain constant, as it does for me.

How exclusive can a club of nearly a quarter-billion members be? Bangla is the language of Bangladesh, the eighth most populous nation in the world, and of the Indian state of West Bengal, the second-largest linguistic group in India. Millions more, documented or not, have settled abroad. Impressive numbers aside, every Bengali, to her at least, is a majority of one. We harbor the faith, implanted by myth and history, of our exalted place in the hierarchy of breeding and culture.

To international relief agency workers, Bangla is the mother tongue of esurient poverty, but to the heirs of *shonar bangla,* golden Bengal of harvest-ready paddyfields and fish-filled rivers, it is the mother tongue of poetry, passion and abundance. It is also the language of nostalgia and of tentative hope: nostalgia for the Hindu-Muslim harmony that existed in undivided Bengal before its vindictive partition by the fleeing British; and hope for the shared mother tongue, devotion to the possible tomorrow that will transcend the religious furies exploited by today's politicians. I think a shared language is stronger than divisive religions. (Based on my travels in Bangladesh, I think Hindu and Muslim Bengalis could cross the abyss between them. It's the national politics of India and corrupt fiefdoms in Bangladesh that get in the way.)

Up to age eight, I lived exclusively in Bangla. My father was the sole support of forty to fifty relatives, who lived with us crowded together in the ground-floor apartment of a two-storied house in a homogenously Hindu, Bangla-speaking, middle-class neighborhood of Kolkata (until recently mispronounced and misspelled as Calcutta by colonialists). All the adults in our large household had been born in villages or towns in the Dhaka (then "Dacca") district of East Bengal (now Bangladesh); all their children, my sisters and cousins, in the thriving capital, Kolkata, in West Bengal. Among themselves, the adults spoke the dialect of Dhaka, the children the Bangla of Kolkata. I had no idea as a child that linguists considered the Dhaka dialect "deviant," and Kolkata the standard. In our home the Dhaka dialect, bangal, was the language of authenticity. You are what dialect your forefathers spoke even if you yourself have lost fluency in it because of successive migrations. We were East Bengalis or *Bangal* first, then Bengali. We distanced ourselves from West Bengalis or *Ghoti* who surrounded us and considered us interlopers. We conducted ourselves as *Bangal*, exiled permanently from our ancestral homeland.

To be born a displaced *Bangal* was to inherit loss of, and longing for, one's true home. Identity had to do with mother tongue, but home was the piece of land that our forefathers had owned, the soil that they had slept and walked on. To be cast out of your *janma bhumi* or ancestral birth-soil is to be forever doomed. Unlike dialects, which can be transported by migrants, the loss of *janma bhumi* is permanent. The diasporic Bengali may own real estate in the country of her adoption, but that real estate can only be her residence, as provisional as her immigrant identity, her home. I think now that this intimate braiding of inherited language, place and identity is why Bengalis never took to the British system of primogeniture. Generation by generation, the extent of ancestral land owned by an individual male was whittled down to specks and strips. It didn't matter that the shrunken land was unprofitable for cultivation and support of large families. Second, third, fourth . . . eighth, ninth. Sons didn't emigrate; they just stayed and got poorer. Evaluation was symbolic, not economic.

Even as a child I picked up on our linguistic nuancing of house *(basha, bari )*, room *(ghar)*, land *(jomi)*, soil *(bhumi)* and homeland *(desh)*. My cousins and I were alert to the moral of the countless children's stories about villagers willing to starve rather than sell off inherited strips of *bhumi*. The most menacing refrain from a popular poem we learned by rote was a rich, greedy landowner's threatening a desperately poor farmer, "Do you get it, Upen / I'm going to buy up your land." Even now in comfortable San Francisco, with every mortgage and property tax payment, I can be thrown into panic by that simple refrain. (Refinance? Never! Lock it in and forget about it, like immigrants or Depression-era survivors who distrust banks.) The inherited culture insists that accidents of impulse and geography have made homelessness my permanent condition; the adopted culture tries to persuade me that home is where I choose to invest love and loyalty.

Better colleges, better job opportunities, natural disasters like floods and famines, and periodic flarings of Hindu-Muslim antagonism had induced my parents' immediate families to migrate to Kolkata in the 1920s and 1930s, though they still owned land in their hometowns. My father had been sent to Kolkata to stay with a childless aunt and uncle-in-law so that he could get a sound English-language undergraduate education at St. Xavier's College, run by Jesuits from Belgium. By then a scholarship student, he stayed for graduate degrees in applied chemistry. After that, as the most educated though not the eldest of nine sons, he dutifully looked for a job in Kolkata, the most prosperous of Bengal's cities. Dependents and family friends also in need of free food and lodging started arriving from the east as soon as they'd heard that he was job-hunting. For a while, the houseguests commuted from Kolkata to their homes in provincial towns of eastern Bengal, where they still jointly owned an ancestral strip.

The Hindu-Muslim riots of 1946, the fiercest in communal

memory, drove the last of the Mukherjee clan out of their home-town, where Muslims constituted an overwhelming majority. The refugees brought with them tales of arson, rape and looting. From their tears and nightmare-hour screams, I learned the special resonance that *bhoi,* the Bangla word for fear, carries. There is no English equivalence for the scale of terror that *bhoi* implies. In words such as *bhoi,* the individual experience of fear is shot through with the memory of unspeakable communal suffering. The partitioning of Bengal in 1947 transformed my vast, extended family from commuters shuttling between residence of convenience and homeland to political refugees stranded in a city where they could never belong. Kolkata was their be-grudged place of asylum.

That exilic melancholy was passed on to me in infancy. We refugees were different from, and superior to, *Ghoti* Bengalis. Which end of the soft-boiled egg do you crack, and should we go to war over it? We rejected matchmaking between *Ghoti* families and ours. We made fun of the *Ghoti* inability to pronounce the "l" sound in *lebu* (lemon) and *loochi* (deep-fried bread). When-ever the East Bengal soccer team played Mohun Bagan, the West Bengal team, we conducted ourselves not as well-brought-up young women but as rowdy soccer fans. The *Ghoti,* in turn, stereotyped us as provincial bumpkins. We directed our Us-versus-Them pugnacity to people who spoke dialects other than the Dhaka one within the *Bangal* community. Long before I had heard of Freud, I had enacted "the narcissism of small differences."

In our house, bangal was the language of passion and of disci-pline. Unhappy wives threatened death by fasting in bangal; virtuous virgins gossiped about neighborhood sluts in it; headstrong young uncles swore at each other in it. Whenever my father had to assume the unwelcome role of patriarch and punish unseemly behavior by a relative, he first, in bangal, consulted his widowed mother, an autocratic upholder of conservative traditions. I remember bangal, however, mainly for the ancient doggerels that my paternal grandmother's coterie of tobacco-chewing, osteoporosis-bent widows recited for their deft delivery of sexist cruelty. Day in and day out, these widows tormented my mother for having borne three daughters and no sons. I may be walking on Haight Street, but I still hear them repeat their malicious couplets: *Puter mutey kori / Meyer galai dori* (There's money to be made off a son's piss / There's rope to hang a daughter with).

My mother tongue transmitted unambiguously the society's values and taboos. Literacy turned women rebellious, unsubmissive, and unmarriageable. My mother, who had been married off the moment she had finished high school, was abused regularly by her in-laws, first for daring to express the hope that she might enroll in a women's college, and later for wanting to send her three daughters to the best elementary school for girls, which happened not to be in our neighborhood. There were harangues and beatings. I didn't realize at the time that I was not just a child-spectator of a scene of authorized sado-masochism, but that I was witness to the last chapters of a long, cultural mega-upheaval. Only very recently, while researching the battle between the Hinducentric traditionalists and the Europhilic reformists (the Brahmo-Samaj) for a novel, I came across a doggerel that has relocated those childhood scenes of pain inflicted and pain accepted in the context of nationalist struggles. *Likhey porey ranhr / buley jano udome shanhr.*

The doggerel is in a colloquial Bangla long out of usage.

*An educated woman is a woman without a husband / Like an untethered ox, she roams around.* On the surface, its moral is familiar and unambiguous: educated women threaten tradition. But the literal translation does not convey the anonymous versifier's hidden linguistic ambiguities and cultural codes. *Ranhr* describes a husbandless woman, who might be a widow (an unfortunate fate in a society that advocates *sati*), or an unmarried woman (a worse fate in a society that expects a woman to worship God through worshipping her husband), or a prostitute. The adjective *udome* that characterizes the ox of the doggerel's analogy can be correctly translated as both "untied" and "naked." *Buley* is the third-person conjugation of the verb *bula* (to roam, loiter, barge in). These ambiguities evoke malicious connections between a woman allowed to learn the three Rs and a loitering whore, who preys on the very society that has cast her out. But, for the Bangla-speaker, this pejorative connotation is undermined or even negated by the great medieval Bengali poet Govinda Das's application of the verb *bula* to the wanderings of poets. In our linguistic community, the poet or *kavi* is not only an artist and entertainer, as she or he might be in the West; the poet is the visionary revealer of ultimate cosmic mysteries. I inherited a mother tongue charged with contradictions and nuances. The capacity of diction to imply opposite meanings has fed me even as I write fiction in English.

(Bangla is not unique in that regard. An Israeli poet friend of my husband's, Ronny Someck, once described modern Hebrew as an amalgam of two sources: the ancient Bible and the modern army. According to him, many words and most poems in that language can be read in at least two ironic, sometimes comic and often-pornographic ways.)

So it was that through *chhara* (lullabies), proverbs, and do-

mestic squabbles, I intuited the dues and privileges of membership in the Bangla-speakers' club. My formal training in ladylike
behavior was undertaken by my paternal grandmother (the
same full-throated widow who harangued my mother for wanting to educate us sisters). She herself had been taught to read as
a child by her older sister, a childless woman whose husband—
picked out by my paternal great-grandfather for his potential to
earn a good living as a doctor in Kolkata—turned out to have progressive ideas. Every night, though we children would have preferred to listen to ghost stories told with dramatic sound effect
by a retired servant who had stayed on with us, this grandmother
recited episodes from the Bangla-version of the *Ramayana* and
the *Mahabharata*.

Of the two epics, the *Ramayana* was my favorite. What young
girl could not thrill to the sheer romance? The handsome and
virtuous prince, Ram, legal heir to the throne of his polyga-
mous father, is banished to the forest. His aged father is in thrall
to a young wife with ambitions to get her own issue appointed
as crown prince. (Didn't we know such stories from the neighborhood, or, indeed, from our own family?) The subsequent
adventures of the banished Ram include wife kidnapping and
Homeric-scale war for wife-rescuing, martial victory and the
final installation of Ram the rightful king. How pale in comparison are Helen and Paris, Greece and Troy. It's *such* a good story,
with its incorporation of shape-changing demons and deities
into everyday reality. I thrilled to the narrative clutter, the strong
plot and the balancing of violence and tenderness. And under all
the convolutions and endless adumbration, it is true to the psychological tensions within the extended family. I was already in
training to be a novelist.

As a writer, I'm sometimes taken to task for linking too many narratives, turning family stories into murder mysteries, indulging myself in violence, ramming ancient history into contemporary reality, dipping into voices and situations (the discredited charge of "appropriation") far beyond my personal experience. Well, blame the *Ramayana*.

My habit of scavenging the world's legacy for ideas and for vocabulary, then reshaping them until they comfortably *belong* to me, is something I must have picked up unconsciously, in infancy. For all our proud insistence on exclusivity, Bengalis (particularly those from Kolkata) have absorbed words from peoples we have come into contact with through trade, wars, migration and marriage, without feeling it a violation of our core identity. Persian was the pre-British court language (and still in circulation during the British Raj); therefore, from Persian we have *golap*, the word for rose, and *ostad*, the term for a master musician. Even the famous Anglo-Indian, Victorian word *durbar*, the elaborate imperial tent and ceremonial display of power, and the refreshing drink, *sharbat*, come from Persian. From a long exposure to Portuguese traders came words like *toali* for towel, *janla* for window, *almira* for almirah or large wooden cabinet. From the British, who made "Calcutta" the traditional seat of power, we got the courts, the schools, parks, the museums and luxurious residences. We also got the first brush with the authority of the English language—and two hundred years' indoctrination in our backwardness. Indianized English words, such as *tebil* for table, *pulish* for police, *kabard* for cupboard, and (my favorite) *tikoji* for tea-cozy, trail a certain colonial shame. Other aspects of the

British linguistic presence, which I will return to later, are far more interesting, or damaging, according to one's interpretation.

In our home, we operated in two distinct forms of Bangla. We spoke chalit or colloquial Bangla, which was peppered with Indianized foreign words that over centuries had lost their foreignness, but when we wrote letters or school essays, we switched to sudha or pure Bangla, which was weighted with Sanskritized words and literary formality. The choice of colloquial or literary depended on the when, why and with whom we needed to communicate. As a child I accepted the uncrossable immensity of the gulf between the oral and the written. It wasn't until I returned from three years of elementary school in England, where I'd had to learn English from scratch in a hurry and to turn in weekly essays on walks taken, birds sighted, holidays in Margate (which I had written in the simple English I spoke and for which I had received top grades), that I rebelled against the Bangla tradition of treating the colloquial as an inferior form unfit for the page.

I was eight when I was initiated into bilingualism. At the school in Sloane Square, I spoke the English I heard around me. At home I spoke the Bangla I had in our Kolkata house. My *Bangal* identity was not at all threatened by my growing fluency in the former colonizer's language. The shock came from suddenly seeing myself as a minority, a brown girl in a white school. I was still a member of the world's most elite linguistic club, but nobody in school knew that.

Within the first weeks of my immersion in English I realized that the Bangla alphabet was far larger. English letters were

arranged higgledy-piggledy, without logical sequence, conform-
ing to no order but the arbitrary "alphabetical." Bangla orders
its vowels separately from its consonants. And when it comes
to consonants, we owned sounds that no English schoolgirl, or
teacher, could copy. The "Bh" in my name, Bharati, was unpronounceable. The nasalizations could not be copied. Consonants
were arranged in rows according to where inside the mouth the
tongue positioned itself. We had three distinct "n" sounds, three
distinct "r" sounds, and though this precision made dictation
exercises very stressful, I began to take pride in the lingual dex-
terity that this precision demanded.

In contrast, English had too thrifty an alphabet. It tolerated
imprecise noises uttered by the lazy-tongued. English had no
use for the nuanced nailing of extended-family relationships.
Their "aunts" and "uncles" seemed disrespectful and generic
compared to our "father's-side older brother" or "mother's second sister." Next to the drawn-out vowels that made spoken
Bangla a euphonic language, English sounded harshly energetic.
I missed the onomatopoeic phrases in Bangla that mimicked
the blowing of wind, the drizzle of rain and gurgle of water-
falls. I missed, too, the echo words (sometimes as ingenious and
coded as cockney rhyming slang), the repetitions—such as *garam
garam,* hot hot (and its infinite expansion: good good, rich rich,
fat fat)—that emphasize caution, respect or possible ridicule. In
English, such repetition comes across as simple-mindedness,
proto–Peter Sellers. Other forms of repetition, like *bosta phosta,*
bags and baggage, vary the initial consonant for a dismissive
implication. My father was a master of the colloquial Bangla put-
down, even while introducing us to distinguished visitors. By the
simple act of artful doubling, he could slip across the counter-

intelligence that Mr. So-and-So had earned his money dishonestly, had wastrel sons and a spendthrift wife.

I envied the English their recording of time passing. They used "yesterday," "today" and "tomorrow" to mark the past, the present and the future while in Bangla we made use of "kal" (time) for all three tenses. My British school chums and I had fundamentally opposed views of Time (also "kal," movement). And as I began to become more fluent in my second language, I became conscious of their syntactical differences. Where my English friends said, " I'm going now" or "I'm reading," in Bangla I would have to say, "I now am going" or "I a book am reading." My brain felt hardwired for constructing sentences in the order my mother tongue dictated.

I began to invest in mother-tongue nostalgia for the story-telling hour with my grandmother and the rowdiness of the relatives who, in Kolkata, I had hidden under beds to avoid. That synthetic nostalgia somehow quickened into a deep longing for the dramatic tales that my mother used to tell about daring young freedom-fighting martyrs from ancestral towns like ours. She told these stories as I ate dinner, sitting on a braided-bamboo mat on the floor along with my many live-in cousins and two sisters. Because of the size of our extended family, we ate in batches: children first, then adult male relatives, then women relatives, then servants. As we ate, my mother, a kavi-seer in her way, launched into stories of teenage boys and girls risking torture in prison, banishment to the penal Andaman Islands and death by hanging in order to take over a police station or an armory. My mother extracted long, pearly bones by macerating chunks of curried carp and then hand-fed me rice and fish balls. She had to make herself heard above squabblers' cries of "I want the fish head!" and "No, it's my turn. You had the head last night. It's not fair, just because my father doesn't . . . ," and the shrill calls of birds settling for the night in the foliage of deodar trees lining the sidewalk.

In the Kolkata remembered oceans away, twilight was a hinge-moment between professing trust in the values of imported Enlightenment and submitting to invisible, cosmic forces. My mother was a skillful deliverer of tales, an improviser (like jazz musicians, I think now) who could keep me tense, entranced, through each re-telling and make the tale's familiar ending come off as unpredictable. Her voice melted my physical surroundings.

As a novelist, I now melt down the cultural borders of my legacies. The fluid concept of time inherited through Bangla's use of *kal* and the "magic realism" inherited from the Hindu epics inform my writing about immigrants in North American cities. Now I write in my third language, American, another "deviant dialect" of the E. M. Forsterian British I learned as authoritative, and in which, in fact, I wrote my first novel and earliest stories.

My mother tongue was a linguistic primer, a thin white-wash over all that is pre-conscious and pre-rational. It was in English that I began to analogize. Successive coats of French and English have faceted Bangla, but it still shines through. It is the odd fate of so many of us in the global community, not just those of us from India but from other homelands at ease in family-time and epic storytelling, that a second language, a school language, was necessary to liberate their minds from their bodies, their self from their community.

Two selves exist within the language-adoptee, as with any adoptee—what might have been, what was lost, and the good fortune, the delivery from want and frustration. For a writer, the melting of a mother tongue is the madeleine, the way back, and the way in, an early loss with the deepest memory, the mother of all plots.

# Yes and No

## Amy Tan

Once, at a family dinner in San Francisco, my mother whispered to me: "Sau-sau [Brother's Wife] pretends too hard to be polite! Why bother? In the end, she always takes everything."

My mother thinks like a *waixiao*, an expatriate, temporarily away from China since 1949, no longer patient with ritual courtesies. As if to prove her point, she reached across the table to offer my elderly aunt from Beijing the last scallop from the Happy Family seafood dish.

Sau-sau scowled. *"B'yao, zhen b'yao!"* (I don't want it, really I don't!) she cried, patting her plump stomach.

"Take it! Take it!" scolded my mother in Chinese.

"Full, I'm already full," Sau-sau protested weakly, eyeing the beloved scallop.

"Ai!" exclaimed my mother, completely exasperated. "Nobody else wants it. If you don't take it, it will only rot!"

At this point, Sau-sau sighed, acting as if she were doing my mother a big favor by taking the wretched scrap off her hands.

My mother turned to her brother, a high-ranking communist official who was visiting her in California for the first time: "In America a Chinese person could starve to death. If you say you don't want it, they won't ask you again forever."

My uncle nodded and said he understood fully: Americans take things quickly because they have no time to be polite.

I thought about this misunderstanding again—of social contexts failing in translation—when a friend sent me an article from the *New York Times Magazine*. The article, on changes in New York's Chinatown, made passing reference to the inherent ambivalence of the Chinese language.

Chinese people are so "discreet and modest," the article stated, there aren't even words for "yes" and "no."

That's not true, I thought, although I can see why an outsider might think that. I continued reading.

If one is Chinese, the article went on to say, "One compromises, one doesn't hazard a loss of face by an overemphatic response."

My throat seized. Why do people keep saying these things? As if we truly were those little dolls sold in Chinatown tourist shops, heads bobbing up and down in complacent agreement to anything said!

I worry about the effect of one-dimensional statements on the unwary and guileless. When they read about this so-called vocabulary deficit, do they also conclude that Chinese people evolved into a mild-mannered lot because the language only allowed them to hobble forth with minced words?

Something enormous is always lost in translation. Something insidious seeps into the gaps, especially when amateur linguists continue to compare, one-for-one, language differences and then put forth notions wide open to misinterpretation: that Chinese people have no direct linguistic means to make decisions, assert or deny, affirm or negate, just say no to drug dealers, or behave properly on the witness stand when told, "Please answer yes or no."

Yet one can argue, with the help of renowned linguists, that the Chinese are indeed up a creek without "yes" and "no." Take any number of variations on the old language-and-reality theory stated years ago by Edward Sapir: "Human beings . . . are very much at the mercy of the particular language which has become the medium for their society. . . . The fact of the matter is that the 'real world' is to a large extent built up on the language habits of the group."

This notion was further bolstered by the famous Sapir-Whorf hypothesis, which roughly states that one's perception of the world and how one functions in it depends a great deal on the language used. As Sapir, Whorf, and new carriers of the banner would have us believe, language shapes our thinking, channels us along certain patterns embedded in words, syntactic structures, and intonation patterns. Language has become the peg and the shelf that enables us to sort out and categorize the world. In English, we see "cats" and "dogs"; what if the language had also specified *glatz,* meaning "animals that leave fur on the sofa," and *glotz,* meaning "animals that leave fur and drool on the sofa"? How would language, the enabler, have changed our perceptions with slight vocabulary variations?

And if this were the case—of language being the master of destined thought—think of the opportunities lost from failure to evolve two little words, *yes* and *no,* the simplest of opposites! Ghenghis Khan could have been sent back to Mongolia. Opium wars might have been averted. The Cultural Revolution could have been sidestepped.

There are still many, from serious linguists to pop psychology cultists, who view language and reality as inextricably tied, one being the consequence of the other. We have traversed the range from the Sapir-Whorf hypothesis to est and neurolinguistic programming, which tell us "you are what you say."

I too have been intrigued by the theories. I can summarize, albeit badly, ages-old empirical evidence: of Eskimos and their infinite ways to say "snow," their ability to *see* differences in snowflake configurations, thanks to the richness of their vocabulary, while non-Eskimo speakers like myself founder in "snow," "more snow," and "lots more where that came from."

I too have experienced dramatic cognitive awakenings via the word. Once I added "mauve" to my vocabulary I began to see it everywhere. When I learned how to pronounce *prix fixe,* I ate French food at prices better than the easier-to-say *à la carte* choices.

But just how seriously are we supposed to take this?

Sapir said something else about language and reality. It is the part that often gets left behind in the dot-dot-dots of quotes: " . . . No two languages are ever sufficiently similar to be considered as representing the same social reality. The worlds in which different societies live are distinct worlds, not merely the same world with different labels attached."

When I first read this, I thought, Here at last is validity for the dilemmas I felt growing up in a bicultural, bilingual family! As any child of immigrant parents knows, there's a special kind of double bind attached to knowing two languages. My parents, for example, spoke to me in both Chinese and English; I spoke back to them in English.

"Amy-ah!" they'd call to me.

"What?" I'd mumble back.

"Do not question us when we call," they scolded me in Chinese. "It is not respectful."

"What do you mean?"

"Ai! Didn't we just tell you not to question?"

To this day, I wonder which parts of my behavior were shaped by Chinese, which by English. I am tempted to think, for example, that if I am of two minds on some matter it is due to the richness of my linguistic experiences, not to any personal tendencies toward wishy-washiness. But which mind says what?

Was it perhaps patience—developed through years of deciphering my mother's fractured English—that had me listening politely while a woman announced over the phone that I had won one of five valuable prizes? Was it respect—pounded in by the Chinese imperative to accept convoluted explanations—that had me agreeing that I might find it worthwhile to drive seventy-five miles to view a time-share resort? Could I have been at a loss for words when asked, "Wouldn't you like to win a Hawaiian cruise or perhaps a fabulous Star of India designed exclusively by Carter and Van Arpels?"

And when this same woman called back a week later, this time complaining that I had missed my appointment, obviously it was my type A language that kicked into gear and interrupted her. Certainly, my blunt denial—"Frankly I'm not interested"—was as American as apple pie. And when she said, "But it's in Morgan Hill," and I shouted, "Read my lips. I don't care if it's Timbuktu," you can be sure I said it with the precise intonation expressing both cynicism and disgust.

It's dangerous business, this sorting out of language and behavior. Which one is English? Which is Chinese? The categories manifest themselves: passive and aggressive, tentative and assertive, indirect and direct. And I realize they are just variations of the same theme: that Chinese people are discreet and modest.

Reject them all!

If my reaction is overly strident, it is because I cannot come across as too emphatic. I grew up listening to the same lines over and over again, like so many rote expressions repeated in an English phrase-book. And I too almost came to believe them.

Yet if I consider my upbringing more carefully, I find there was nothing discreet about the Chinese language I grew up with. My parents made everything abundantly clear. Nothing wishy-washy in their demands, no compromises accepted: "Of course you will become a famous neurosurgeon," they told me. "And yes, a concert pianist on the side."

In fact, now that I remember, it seems that the more emphatic outbursts always spilled over into Chinese: "Not that way! You must wash rice so not a single grain spills out."

I do not believe that my parents—both immigrants from Mainland China—are an exception to the modest-and-discreet rule. I have only to look at the number of Chinese engineering students skewing minority ratios at Berkeley, MIT, and Yale. Certainly they were not raised by passive mothers and fathers who said, "It's up to you, my daughter. Writer, welfare recipient, masseuse, or molecular engineer—you decide."

And my American mind says, See, those engineering students weren't able to say no to their parents' demands. But then my Chinese mind remembers: Ah, but those parents all wanted their sons and daughters to be *pre-med*.

Having listened to both Chinese and English, I also tend to be suspicious of any comparisons between the two languages. Typically, one language—that of the person doing the comparing—is often used as the standard, the benchmark for a logical form of expression. And so the language being compared is always in danger of being judged deficient or superfluous, simplistic or un-necessarily complex, melodious or cacophonous. English speakers point out that Chinese is extremely difficult because it relies on variations in tone barely discernible to the human ear. By the same token, Chinese speakers tell me English is extremely difficult because it is inconsistent, a language of too many broken rules, of Mickey Mice and Donald Ducks.

Even more dangerous to my mind is the temptation to compare both language and behavior *in translation.* To listen to my mother speak English, one might think she has no concept of past or future tense, that she doesn't see the difference between singular and plural, that she is gender blind because she calls my husband "she." If one were not careful, one might also generalize that, based on the way my mother talks, all Chinese people take a circumlocutory route to get to the point. It is, in fact, my mother's idiosyncratic behavior to ramble a bit.

I worry that the dominant society may see Chinese people from a limited—and limiting—perspective. I worry that seemingly benign stereotypes may be part of the reason there are few Chinese in top management positions, in mainstream political roles. I worry about the power of language: that if one says anything enough times—in *any* language—it might become true.

Could this be why Chinese friends of my parents' generation are willing to accept the generalization?

"Why are you complaining?" one of them said to me. "If people think we are modest and polite, let them think that. Wouldn't Americans be pleased to admit they are thought of as polite?"

And I do believe anyone would take the description as a compliment—at first. But after a while, it annoys, as if the only things that people heard one say were phatic remarks: "I'm so pleased to meet you. I've heard many wonderful things about you. For me? You shouldn't have!"

These remarks are not representative of new ideas, honest

emotions, or considered thought. They are what is said from the polite distance of social contexts: of greetings, farewells, wedding thank-you notes, convenient excuses, and the like.

It makes me wonder, though. How many anthropologists, how many sociologists, how many travel journalists have documented so-called "natural interactions" in foreign lands, all observed with spiral notebook in hand? How many other cases are there of the long-lost primitive tribe, people who turned out to be sophisticated enough to put on the stone-age show that ethnologists had come to see?

And how many tourists fresh off the bus have wandered into Chinatown expecting the self-effacing shopkeeper to admit under duress that the goods are not worth the price asked? I have witnessed it.

"I don't know," the tourist said to the shopkeeper, a Cantonese woman in her fifties. "It doesn't look genuine to me. I'll give you three dollars."

"You don't like my price, go somewhere else," said the shopkeeper.

"You are not a nice person," cried the shocked tourist, "not a nice person at all!"

"Who say I have to be nice," snapped the shopkeeper.

"So how does one say 'yes' and 'no' in Chinese?" my friends ask a bit warily.

And here I do agree in part with the *New York Times Magazine* article. There is no one word for "yes" or "no" —but not out of necessity to be discreet. If anything, I would say the Chinese equivalent of answering "yes" or "no" is di*screte,* that is, specific to what is asked.

Ask a Chinese person if he or she has eaten, and he or she might say *chrle* (eaten already) or perhaps *meiyou* (have not).

Ask, "So you had insurance at the time of the accident?" and the response would be *dwei* (correct) or *meiyou* (did not have).

Ask, "Have you stopped beating your wife?" and the answer refers directly to the proposition being asserted or denied: stopped already, still have not, never beat, have no wife.

What could be clearer?

As for those who are still wondering how to translate the language of discretion, I offer this personal example.

My aunt and uncle were about to return to Beijing after a three-month visit to the United States. On their last night I announced I wanted to take them out to dinner.

"Are you hungry?" I asked in Chinese.

"Not hungry," said my uncle promptly, the same response he once gave me ten minutes before he suffered a low blood-sugar attack.

"Not too hungry," said my aunt. "Perhaps you're hungry?"

"A little," I admitted.

"We can eat, we can eat then," they both consented.

"What kind of food?" I asked.

"Oh, doesn't matter. Anything will do. Nothing fancy, just some simple food is fine."

"Do you like Japanese food? We haven't had that yet," I suggested.

They looked at each other.

"We can eat it," said my uncle bravely, this survivor of the Long March.

"We have eaten it before," added my aunt. "Raw fish."

"Oh, you don't like it?" I said. "Don't be polite. We can go somewhere else."

"We are not being polite. We can eat it," my aunt insisted.

So I drove them to Japantown and we walked past several restaurants featuring colorful plastic displays of sushi.

"Not this one, not this one either," I continued to say, as if searching for a Japanese restaurant similar to the last. "Here it is," I finally said, turning into a restaurant famous for its Chinese fish dishes from Shandong Province.

"Oh, Chinese food!" cried my aunt, obviously relieved.

My uncle patted my arm. "You think like a Chinese."

"It's your last night here in America," I said. "So don't be polite. Act like an American."

And that night we ate a banquet.

# Trouble with Language

## Josef Škvorecký

I'm told that the first decade of life decides life for as many decades as it takes a man to return to his Maker. Judging by the evidence of my life, I believe it's true.

I was born in a small town built on an ancient route through a pass between two mountain ranges by which caravans of merchants entered the vast valley of Bohemia, reaching eventually its heart. In the times of the Celts and the Germans it was just a fortress, Marobudum, but after the influx of Slavic tribes it grew into a town, then city, then metropolis called Prague. On medieval maps the mountain pass was called *Porta regni*, the Gate to the Kingdom, i.e., the kingdom of the mightiest tribe in the region, the Czechs.

When I was a child, America was far, very far away: only an echo of some unreachable reality. And yet, my earliest cultural memory came from that misty midregion of Weir. Sitting on my mother's lap in the local cinema, a mere pre-schooler, I saw Fatty Arbuckle's two-reeler *Saved by Fido* and I remembered it, in the twisted memory of a child, till the day some sixty years later, in Canada, when I read a book on Hollywood silent comedies.

My second cultural inspiration came also from North America; this time, however, it was literary. The author of the book was an American from Michigan, James Oliver Curwood, and the novel was *Men of Brave Hearts* (I hope that was the title—I'm translating from my Czech memory). It was the first part of a trilogy set in the Canadian North, with Mounties as heroes, chasing (and saving) beautiful Indian girls—the Rose Marie stuff. My father gave it to me for Christmas—in those days principal Christmas presents were not toy cars but books. I was to wait but didn't till next Christmas for further adventures of Mounties and their paramours. I bought the second part myself, out of savings from my weekly allowance, but to my dismay at the end of the book I found the publisher's note that, regrettably, Mr. Curwood died suddenly without finishing his trilogy.

Here fate intervened. I sat down and finished the saga for the late Mr. Curwood: *The Mysterious Cave,* my opus number one. Father was so impressed by the eighteen-page novel that he typed it up for me and drew a frontispiece. He copied it, on translucent paper, from an illustration in a Karl May novel. In those days novels came out illustrated.

Of course I thought that Mr. Curwood was a Canadian. Who else would write so convincingly about the Canadian wilderness? (Convincingly, that is, for me, who knew a big zero about the wilderness in the north of America.)

Nevertheless, my aroused literary passion didn't end with this mistake. About two years later, the pseudo-Canadian Curwood was replaced in my affection by an American who, unfortunately, *was* Canadian. I don't know why I was convinced that Ernest Thompson Seton was a Yankee, and that *Two Little Savages* was set in Chicago and on a farm nearby. Probably I overheard my mother's visitors discussing the then fashionable translation of an American novel called *The Jungle,* with its gloomy descriptions of life and animal deaths in the Windy City. Ladies in those distant pre-Oprah days sometimes actually discussed books.

Again, it wasn't until some sixty years later, in Toronto, which on a winter day can be pretty gloomy, that I found (in a city guide) that the Don Valley, some ten minutes' walk from our house, was the scene of Seton's young hero's depressed roamings in the deep forests around the gloomy city; that Ian lived in my adoptive home of Toronto, not in Illinois; and that Seton was not an American.

Later, in another chapter of my early life, I almost died of pneumonia—as with nearly everything in my childhood, it was in some sort of "pre" days; in this case, pre-antibiotics—and consequently, when I miraculously survived, doctor's orders excluded me from participation in boys' sports, of which, before my illness, I had been an avid enthusiast. I even dreamed of introducing rugby football to my school. Arbuckle, Curwood and Seton had already made me an Anglophile. Rugby had been played in Prague since the mid-nineteenth century but it never gained popularity. After World War Two, when I once went to see a championship game in Prague, there were more people in the field than in the stands. I was sitting there, the lonely man in the company of five or six suffering wives of the diehards who were giving each other bloody noses on the grass.

The rugby dream ended anyway, even without my pneumonia: I was unable to buy a rugby ball. They were not on the market.

Excluded from the companionship of ball-kicking boys, I read. My father's home library provided me with quite a lot of translations because my father followed tradition. The Czech nation, or rather its language, was reborn on translations, mostly of English and American classics. The Czechs had lost the ancient sovereignty of their kingdom (in the same year that the Pilgrim Fathers landed in America), and with it—almost—its language, too. Reading those precious and very bad translations, I shook with horror with A. G. Pym on the hull of the capsized *Grampus*; I did things I never dared to do otherwise with Penrod; I sailed down the mystery of the Mississippi, through incomprehensible bloody feuds between the Grangerfords and the Shepherdsons; I flew in a balloon over the Sahara desert with Tom Sawyer, and, yes, I also felt the unoppressive humidity of the tropical forest where Tarzan lived with his family of apes. My *education sentimentale*.

Thanks to this abundance of translated novels I had no need of English, which was not taught at the gymnasium. There we had to master Latin, German and French, this last the "language of diplomats." Before WWII this may have been true; English certainly wasn't the *lingua franca* of the world, as it is nowadays.

Then biology interfered. My glands began to do their disturbing work and I fell in love with an American boy. Actually he was British, which I again didn't know, for he lived in Hollywood, California. His name was Freddie Bartholomew and, at a Sunday afternoon matinee in the same cinema where I had seen Arbuckle from my mother's lap, I saw Freddie in *Little Lord Fauntleroy*. Many if not all young boys, I'm told, go through an early homosexual phase. Mine was strictly an affair of the soul, and anyway, I was saved from the then very sad fate of a gay person by an unquestionable female, also from Hollywood, named Judy Garland. I jilted Freddie for her after I'd heard her singing in the race-track drama *Thoroughbreds Don't Cry*.

The platonic affair had a side effect; I decided to learn English so as to be able to write Judy a love-letter. Which at long last brings me to my theme.

I acquired a little pocketbook entitled *Teach Yourself English* and became deeply immersed in Judy's tongue. I was an only child in a relatively affluent family and my parents believed in easing the burden of school mass instruction by hiring private tutors for me. One day, my French tutor, Mrs. Hlavackova, called on my mother with sad news: she, asserted the French lady, had never had such a stupid pupil as I was. (Only she said "untalented.") It would be a sorry waste of money to continue paying for my French lessons.

Mother was not pleased; however, she found my little English textbook, and instead of punishing me, she provided me with another private teacher, Miss Pokorna, to instruct me in English. She was a wise lady, my poor mother—dead at fifty from high blood pressure, which I was diagnosed with at fifty and, at seventy-eight, I'm still here. She died in another one of those "pre" times.


I can't resist a digression. The most beloved of my private language tutors was Mr. Neu, the cantor of the local synagogue, who taught me to speak an almost perfect German. His first name dated also from the "pre" days, for his parents innocently named him Adolf. He perished in Theresienstadt. Before he died, in the twilight days when Jews in my native town were still allowed the luxury of a "Jewish Café," our German lessons changed into nostalgic meditations of the past. *"Was wir Juden schon alles mitgemacht haben!"* sighed Mr. Neu, and then he would tell me about the days of World War One, which were also bad; there was very little food, but he would give private German lessons and refused to be paid in money, though he accepted *Zucker, Mehl, sogar Fleisch.* The German he taught was radically different from the one I used to hear later, in the Messerschmitt factory, or watching the weekly Ufa newsreels in the local cinema. The Big Boss of Czech schools in those days was one Inspektor Werner, whose method of inspection was to burst unexpectedly in on a teacher unprepared for the horror, listen for half an hour to his stuttering instruction, then attack him with language best characterized by the tubercular Mr. Propilek, a teacher of Russian and Baltic languages (which, naturally, were not taught in the Protektorate). He once underwent the trial of the scowling brows of Inspektor Werner, then the explosion of his gutter diatribe. But when Inspektor Werner briefly stopped to catch his breath, Mr. Propilek made the memorable pronouncement of: *Ich lehre Goethes Deutsch, Herr Inspektor. Ich lehre nicht Schweindeutsch.* This, miraculously, made the bloodthirsty Nazi shut up. Inspektor Werner survived Mr. Neu by a mere couple of years. After the war's end they hanged him.

Mr. Propilek was later banned from teaching Russian by the Commies.

Next to Mr. Neu in my affection was my gymnasium German instructor, Dr. Eva Althammer, a pretty young blonde, an *echt Deutsch* with a quintessentially Aryan name. She, however, never joined the Nazis, loved Rilke, and married a man by the name of Svorcik. Thus she committed minor *Rassenschande,* and because she refused to join the party and her husband wouldn't change his nationality to German, with an appropriate change of the orthography of his name, Inspektor Werner threatened her with Ravensbrück. Werner's threats were never to be taken lightly; some people paid with their life for such mistakes. So Mrs. Althammer-Svorcik turned to a friend of my father's, a Czech doctor, who advised her to get pregnant. The Nazis, he correctly maintained, in their twisted race theory, wouldn't send an innocent unborn German baby to a concentration camp. Before Werner's threats, she and her husband intended to wait for peace to have babies, but now she followed the doctor's advice and survived. Many years later, when she became my first German translator, I gave her the only poem I wrote in German, when I was her admiring pupil in the Quinta—a gross imitation of her beloved Rainer Maria Rilke:

*Bald kommen Winterstürme mit dem weissen Schneen*
*Und langsam wird zum Koder alte liebe Pfad.*
*In meinem Herze kalte Winde wehen . . .*

Back to my English beginnings. About a year after she'd hired Miss Pokorna, my mother enquired about my progress. Miss Pokorna with great enthusiasm assured her that I was her best student ever.

My English was a labor of love.

By the way, I managed to send the love-letter to Judy on December 2nd, 1941. By that time we no longer lived in Czechoslovakia but were second-rate citizens of the Protektorate Böhmen und Mähren in the German Reich. Mail to America, however, was still functioning; the States were not to join the war until a few days later. Chances are that Judy got my letter. In any case, she never answered, but soon I didn't mind. Local beauties were replacing Judy in my heart.

And with Miss Pokorna I read my first English and American writers in the original tongue. My tutor was a graduate of a British boarding school attended when her father was stationed in London as a business representative of some sort, and so her English was real. Why her family had returned to Czechoslovakia a few days before it was annexed by the Reich I don't know. In those days very few people had an idea of the bottomless evil that was Hitler.

She had a good private library of English and American authors, and after I quickly mastered basic grammar, she made me read Shaw, O'Neill, Oscar Wilde, Kipling, Mark Twain and O. Henry.

I was sixteen, seventeen, the author already of several unfinished early novels about the glorious career of a Czech saxophonist in Hollywood nightclubs, and the author also of a more mature and finished (though unpublished) novel called *An Inferiority Complex*. It featured the heroines of my later novels Irena and Marie, and also the Kostelec jazz band.

Like every young person, I avidly read poems: the poets of the Czech "poetism" movement, Karel Čapek's unique translations of modern French poetry. Miss Pokorna lent me a volume of T. S. Eliot. The war was going badly for the Reich; that meant it was going well for us involuntary citizens, and I was drafted into the *Totaleinsatz* in a Messerschmitt subsidiary which manufactured fighter planes and Stukas. There, against the background noises of drills and pneumatic hammers, I recited to myself:

> *Because I do not hope to turn again*
> *Because I do not hope*
> *Because I do not hope to turn*

I do not pretend that I understood the meaning of Eliot's verses. But they had a quality of magic incantation—probably my first touch of the magic of language.

The war ended, and in a bookstore in Prague I bought a copy of Hemingway's *A Farewell to Arms*, published in Sweden but in English. I read it and I understood what Josef Hora, a Czech poet, had meant when, long before Márquez, he wrote about magic realism in prose. Unlike the Spanish-American leftist, what Hora meant was not introducing supernatural elements in prose, or falsifying historical data to suit one's ideological purpose, but the novelist's duty to take infinitesimal care of each and every word, the way a lyrical poet does.

Reading Hemingway's story of Catherine and Fred, I saw that this was precisely the way Hemingway wrote: the way novels should be written. Henceforth I tried to follow the advice of the poet and the example of the novelist. Many, many years later a Czech literary critic, Premysl Blazicek, very kindly said about my novel *The Bride of Texas* that each sentence in that book was perfect.

Whether he was right or not, I don't dare to judge. What is certain, however, is that no American critic would say that, because they don't know my writings. I mean: they don't know how these books are written since they don't read the obscure language of the westernmost Slavs.

My inner language, since the murky days of sickly adolescence, was English. I even said my evening prayers in that foreign tongue, and I voraciously read books from Miss Pokorna's private library. Years later, as a student of philosophy, I belonged to the privileged few in Stalin's Reich who could get almost all important modern works in the original language from the seminar library of the English department. At the same time, the more I immersed myself in these books, the more I ignored Czech literature. In that respect I probably could be a Guinness laureate. When, at long last, my novel about the Czech Communist Army appeared in America (it was banned in Czechoslovakia, not published there until after the fall of the Evil Empire) and American reviewers made the obvious comparisons to *The Good Soldier Schweik,* I still hadn't read the notorious classic.

Americans are linguistically very tolerant, very nice. I was often congratulated on my very good or even excellent English. On each such occasion I grinned politely because I knew only too well that it was just American politeness. English was still my very limited inner language, grammatically more or less correct, but idiomatic? "Do you now write in English?" was the usual follow-up question. Only articles, I would answer. For writing articles you don't have to be at home in a language. I never dared to say "essays," always "articles," because I painfully felt that for that noble genre my English inner self was lamentably inadequate.

I often remembered the kind Miss Pokorna, long after she got married to a theatrical producer in Prague, long after I started a new and different life in Canada. In her assessment of my linguistic talent, either she was wrong or the English proficiency standards in my native town were comfortably low. True, I learned English rather quickly—to a degree. A degree that enabled me to read books (with and soon without a pocket dictionary) and to discuss them intelligently. Yes, to discuss literature, and that came in handy when I found myself teaching literary courses at the University of Toronto. My abilities in non-literary conversations, such as talking to people in eateries and bars, were, and remained, restricted. In short, I reached some kind of limit, a barrier, a boundary, and I was never able to surmount the obstacle.

I read Conrad because he must have faced a similar problem when, as an adult, he had to learn a foreign language in which he later so incomparably excelled. Graham Greene always maintained that Conrad was the best English stylist of the twentieth century. I read and re-read *Heart of Darkness,* covered with sweat while stumbling through the richness of his vocabulary, awed by the music of the dark sentences. Then, from Ford Madox Ford's memoir, I learned that Conrad's *spoken* English was far from perfect, perhaps not even very good. But what help was it to me? Conrad *did* write like a demiurge. I didn't. Certainly not in my acquired language. In my native language?

A strange thing and Henry Miller got it right. Surrounded by the sounds of the foreign language—speaking, on a daily basis, my very good English, as friends kindly assured me—my eyes, my ears, my inner receptive organs became attuned to Czech to a much higher degree of precision than back in Bohemia. I awakened to aspects of my mother tongue of which formerly I was unaware, having used them subconsciously, mechanically. The sex appeal of feminine endings, the lure of verbal aspects, the capricious scherzos of prefixes, such things.

Nevertheless, I continued to read in English. The magic of Faulkner, the biting manner of Waugh, Chandler's vistas of nature and street, the beauty of the lingo, Hemingway's early hypnotic brevity. Such things. And I wrote.

Did I imitate? Perhaps. If so, only in the sense of *Imitatio Christi,* with language as my religion, as my home. That's why I was never nostalgic. The old country, with its fifty years of non-sensical but cruel dictatorships, was not my home anymore. The language was. Czech. The language of my mother, of my writing.

And yet, prodded by those well-meaning friends, I once tried to cross the barrier and wrote a novel in English. It was a joy to feel the moulding of sentences, of dialogues, of descriptions in an acquired language, with here and there some peach of an idiom, overheard in a pub or maybe suggested by Marlowe—the detective, not the murdered playwright. The joy, as it were, of being an additional human being, because writing in an additional tongue. That joy.

However, it didn't last long. At my publisher's, editor girls went to work and when the book was out, they didn't earn much praise. Something is lost, the reviewers decided. When he writes in English, something is missing. The Genius of Language, perhaps?

Were they right? Don't ask me. What those kind editor girls earned was my admiration, mixed, however, with the bitter feeling of defeat. The girls didn't correct many grammatical errors; they just made my English English. In their hands my vocabulary blossomed to an almost Conradian opulence. Yet these were blossoms created by those girls' hands, not mine.

The reviewers never read my novels as I had written them in my "small"—for most American critics, even "obscure"—language. They read only translations. And I thought of my early days, of the Sinclairs and Dickenses and Dreisers, not to speak of Curwoods and Setons and Edgar Rice Burroughses, all of them enjoyed in dubious—no: bad—no: horrible translations, translations really insulting to sensitive speakers of the obscure language of the westernmost Slavs. And I wondered. What made me enjoy Mr. Babbitt, who constantly used the second person plural in addressing his children, his wife, his closest friends? What made me ignore the shocking impoliteness of characters who addressed their physicians with the disrespectful "Doctor," not "Mr. Doctor"? What made me so imperceptive of the twisted sentences that slavishly followed the word order of the originals? Did they sound alluringly exotic? Sweetly foreign? What made me not wonder about a military band in Thackeray whose bulky musician played very loudly on the dulcimer? All that?

Surely, there was nothing resembling genius in the language of those translations. Yet the novels spoke to me, with great intensity. So strongly that they decided my future. True, there was Eliot, whom I first read in English, then years later in a supposedly good Czech translation, who, after the true magic of "Because I do not hope. . . ," was almost torture. Was it Josef Hora's labor devoted to each word which the translator, paid by that word, obviously neglected? Something else?

For a decade of my life, when my own efforts were banned, I turned translator myself. The experience taught me to appreciate my excellent translators in Canada. I bitterly learned what it was to cleanse your text of the abundance of auxiliary verbs so foreign to Czech, of the prevalence of the passive voice, of possessive pronouns used with parts of the human body, all these and other translators' errors which so uglified the American magic of Faulkner, the British acrimony of Waugh, the translucency of Hemingway's diction. Would any American monolingual or even—in the major languages—bilingual or trilingual reviewer dare to say what the late Czech critic said about my sentences?

No, and it wouldn't be their fault. Although they were unaware of my originals, their reviews were rarely scathing, often favorable. What about language, then? What is it that makes even books that present only a ragged shadow of their model enjoyable, even enthralling? What makes a teenager in a land-locked little country ruled and butchered by foreign invaders and mighty Big Daddies enter the skin of an illiterate boy from Missouri, of a nigger slave—enter a world as far away as the stars?

Yes, language can be of supreme beauty. But there is more to works of fiction than just language. Style in Chandler's sense, the experience of Dickens but also that of Henry James, of life's martyrdom or of life's sweet mellowness, and many other things.

Let's leave it to the horses, they have bigger heads.

Or perhaps to the elephants.

# Circus Biped

## Bert Keizer

*Die Grenze meiner Sprache sind die Grenze meiner Welt,* said Wittgenstein. The limits of my language are the limits of my world. You would almost leap to: my language is my world. An aphasiac's nightmare is the waking-up after a stroke to discover that everybody speaks Chinese. This is the worst possible way of being catapulted into a foreign language, because you find yourself out of a world in a flash.

My journey into English was luckily a much more gradual affair, which started with the trying-on of funny little hats while in the back of my mind there already hovered a mirage of me striding in full regalia down the path toward—oh, I don't know, a beach in California, an Oxford quadrangle, a glen in Scotland, or a pub in Dublin—obvious places, anyway, which in fact I never got to.

The first word was "YES," encountered in a boys' book about cowboys and Indians. White Feather was the stony Indian and Eagle Eye the impetuous cowboy. We pronounced it "coyboy," for some reason, though there was nothing coy in sight, I can assure you. Neither did we connect "cow" to anything bovine, because it is impossible to imagine a daredevil in full gallop swinging a lasso in swirls of dust, amidst excited cries, next to the proverbial sluggishness of a Dutch cow in a dreamy meadow. The poor dears would be very upset at such an unnecessary display of sound and fury, so deeply foreign to their drowsy domain.

But White Feather's YES was emblematic as my first English utterance, charged with sturdy manliness, an inborn determination to remain unruffled (though I am not sure about how far the waves of English commingle here, for it may well be the case that I confuse several avenues down which this language came washing over me). White Feather and Eagle Eye—in Dutch: Witte Veder en Arendsoog—were probably assembled by their author, J. P. Nowee (who from his own experience couldn't tell a cowboy from a parking space), out of the motley crowd that fought its way onto the Normandy beaches in 1944, bringing cigarettes, gum, and a way with the girls, from which assets he picked the boy-ingredients and mixed them up with what he had gathered from the movies about prairies.

YES!

I didn't know how to pronounce it, because I had never seen the letter Y, and inwardly mumbled something like "aye."

In 1952, English to me meant soldiers marching merrily down the road, not your biting Nazi maniacs, but free spirits in good order, always willing to break the ranks for a laugh or a drink, and carrying hardly any bullets in their rifles. "The Yellow Rose of Texas," with the militaristic undertow of the snare drum, was the song for me. Or the melancholy sound of "Tom Dooley." "Hang on your hat, Tom Dooley" is what I heard, because that is closest to the Dutch idiom of placing your hat on a hook. The next phrase sounded to me like "Good boy you're boy goodbye," and on these words the picture arose of a good boy who took off his hat and was sung to by an admiring circle of old wise men. Then Tennessee Ernie Ford's "I owe my soul to the company store," from which I gathered that if you lived long enough in an American wood, you would turn into something like this poor brute who could talk to the world no more, only hammer blows on it.

All this hale-and-heartiness was a far cry from the surly male who next made his entry, and this summing-up inadvertently takes on the obvious hue of my own emerging maleness, which must have traveled down that road from fairy-tale cowboy through adolescent sulk to youthful doubt, ending up in an instant of unquivering certainty (which we'll talk about some other time), and from there on down the relentless slope, struggling fiercely—if only to instill the idea in the audience that I am fighting my way down, not just sliding.

I forgot to mention an all-pervasive and therefore hardly noticeable aspect of all this: the fact that a Dutch boy in the second half of the twentieth century should build up a considerable part of his bulwark against the world using English bricks. Allied bricks.

I even imagined, in that stage when I was feeling myself into the English language, that I could dream up the English equivalent of Dutch words by mentally staring at their essence and transmuting that in the furnace of my inner appreciation into the English expression I was looking for. Somewhere in my mental attic there still subsist the remains of these verbal phantoms, which at the time felt to me like proper English words. This effort at linguistic alchemy, throwing in my Dutch iron in order to extract a nugget of English gold, was not entirely silly, because many Dutch words are entangled with English words—and I am not talking deep linguistics or sophisticated etymology here. What I mean are simple look-alikes or sound-alikes, which were as enticing as they were confusing to a boy not even vaguely in command of words. Consider "girl" and the Dutch equivalent, "meisje." Now, these two words would never run into each other in my mind, but "maid" and "meid" are almost twins in appearance and sound, though wholly different in meaning: "meid" denoting (outside the household) a gal rather than a girl, and gals being more fun, so much fun, even, that a certain boundary may be crossed beyond which a "meid" becomes a hussy.

All this fumbling with English words and sounds is pre-literate and was mainly brought home to me through songs, for I rarely heard English spoken. I cannot remember one word from the Roy Rogers movies we saw, and I only recently discovered that his horse was named Trigger, when I saw a documentary about the famous cowboy in which he proudly sat next to his beloved horse, now in stuffed condition—a bizarre sight that made me uncomfortable for Trigger's sake.

I was raised in a Dutch Roman Catholic family, my mother a farmer's daughter, my father the son of a village painter, the two of them setting up house in a small provincial town in the 1930s. We grew up under the awning of the last vestiges of medieval Christendom. But that's hindsight. Well into the mid-fifties, we were comfortably stuck in a homely nineteenth-century version of the Middle Ages. Dutch Roman Catholicism had retreated into an alley, far away from the busy traffic rushing past on the intellectual highways of Europe. Wittgenstein had died already,

Beckett was approaching Nobel stature, but in our parish the Trinity remained an inscrutable Mystery.

We had no idea we lay under siege. What would have made us think that, anyway? Perry Como didn't sound like much of a threat. Every little statue in our parish church stayed exactly where it was when he sang. I never caught on to pre-Army Elvis, and only realized he was around in his chubby phase. But then, in 1963, the Beatles came along, and under the spell of that sound we forgot all about statues and strolled out of the church with a laugh, being dealt a smart kick in the ass by the Rolling Stones on the threshold, just to make sure. We left our parents sitting there, and for all I know that is where they still linger.

Dutchmen of my generation like to think that they fought themselves free of the clutches of the Church in heroic fashion. As if they entered into a fierce exchange with their elders—nay, with God Himself, preferably—from which, surprisingly, they emerged triumphant. Now, this is more or less how things would have gone if they had woken up in the thirties, where ostracism would have been the reward of anyone dropping out of the sacred community; but in 1963 it was all grassy meadows, "an endless breaking of the bank," that was beckoning us.

The Beatles pulled the rug from under that particular brand of unsmiling masculinity, the D-Day heroes who kept their cigarettes going under enemy fire and never stopped chewing their gum, even while burning thousands of innocent people with their carpet-bombings in Germany. "It was a terrible job but it had to be done." *You can stuff your terrible jobs* is what the Beatles said.

I may have made a hash of Tom Dooley and the Company Store, and only sensed a sunny Sunday's contentment in Magic

Moments, but the Beatles' lyrics I actually understood. "I want to hold your hand" is not exactly unfathomable, though in "Love Me Do" I initially mistook "Do" for a girl's name. It was the Beatles' English that ushered me into the language proper. Before they sang it to me, English was atmosphere, not language as a charged verbal message. From then on, the possibility lurked for me that one day I might say "I" in English.

When I moved to England in 1968, the last strains of Vera Lynn were still in the air—something you wouldn't think when listening to the Stones' "Jumpin' Jack Flash," which came out that summer ("I was drowned with a spike right through my head"). But that was the inexplicable charm of the place in those days. The Second World War was really over, a mere mirage now over the white cliffs of Dover; the last GIs were finally out of the way; and an entirely new way of being young was invented on the spot (I know, but that's how it felt), seemingly out of nothing, and outrageously whipped into a more daring frenzy by the kids of those same GIs, who were about to be slaughtered in Vietnam, which lacked all Normandy glamor.

The first thing that struck me when I moved to England was the fact that youngsters there didn't understand much of Bob Dylan's lyrics either. I reluctantly abandoned my theory that "Like a Rolling Stone" was a tribute to Mick Jagger's way of life, but didn't get much in exchange. I suppose Dylan's texts are still a bit of a problem: shallow nonsense or sheer genius stuff.

Though my brother told me not to (it would spoil everything, especially my "freedom"), I fell, after or while asking many questions, into the arms of the first girl who talked to me for longer than five minutes. She came from London, she lived in Corn-wall, she was doing her A-levels. I was a waiter in the local hotel and spouted English by the mile, sounding awfully American—a remnant of the Continent's debt to our liberators, an accent which was not exactly an endearing asset in those days, because of Vietnam. My surname, which was always pronounced in the "Kaiser Bill" manner, was kindly pardoned as betraying my "Aus-trian" descent, because nobody wanted to besmear me with any German connections, and to the blissfully ignorant people I moved amongst, "Austrian" meant "German, but all right really."

To certain English people, it did seem unlikely that there was such a thing as a Dutch language at all. Once, while having tea in the house of a vicar, father of a friend, I was asked by the wife in the sweetest tones imaginable, "I wonder, do you Dutch have a language?"—by which she sought my confirmation of her opin-ion that probably we merely spoke a ragbag of dialects, assem-bled over the years from passing marauders such as Romans, Celts, Frisians, Vikings, Franks, and Saxons, out of whose verbal droppings we, the local monkeys, somehow fabricated what we took to be a language. This made me so angry that I practically hissed at her: "No, ma'am, we do not have a language, we just bark at each other from the trees!" My friend hastened me into the garden to cool down while his father attended to Mummy, who was quite taken aback by my "vicious and entirely uncalled for snarl."

My girlfriend led me firmly out of sundry other confusions (don't ever try to work out the difference between the *ough* in *plough, rough,* and *thorough,* but do pronounce them differently), reminding me of the old joke that in English words are not written as they are spoken—unlike the case in everyone's native language. I never quite mastered the "th" and sounded unbearably silly while singing along with Mary Hopkin's song, "Dose were de days, my friend." Though I didn't shrink into a mere figure of fun, I certainly became ridiculous in unsought ways by having to plod along in this borrowed garb. Anyone who is not fluent in a strange language sheds about 30 to 40 IQ points; that's quite a dive, which few intellects will be able to sustain without some damage to their underlying ego. Being surrounded by benevolent English speakers, I was quickly helped back on my feet, only to fall into the next trap: idolatry.

It takes a few years to get well acquainted with the clichés in a language, and the list can never be exhaustive, but there is a stage where you are innocent of the difference between a worn-out phrase and a gem of personal expression. So at one stage I found sayings such as *looking like death warmed over, green around the gills, get stuffed, kicked the bucket, deaf as a post,* and *blind as a bat* a delight, until I found them out as the dead doornails they really are.

One thing I picked up very quickly was the possibility of positioning people socially by listening to their language. Gutsy, arrogant, boaster; working-class-and-doomed, working-class-and-angry, working-class-and-on-the-way-up; hardly, reasonably, highly, and over-educated; arty type, peasant—the millions of possibilities according to which we stack people socially, using our judgment or wallowing in prejudice—all that is soon learned in any European language. Mainly, I suspect, because our own tribe consists of similar strata. I mention this because, during my stay as a doctor in Africa, I had to go without all these pointers and could only tell a peasant from a genius by using clothes, body care, and face, which often pointed in the wrong direction.

I cannot remember any half-reading in English, the way I now do in Chateaubriand's *Mémoires d'outre-tombe*, looking up words, pondering phrases, and sometimes not getting anywhere. But I still have my copy of *Ulysses*, read in 1970, my second year in England, and there I have rather annoyingly marked the words I didn't understand. This is what I was stuck with after the first fourteen pages: *threadbare, fretted, breeks, skivvy's, whinge, lunged, rashers, gaud, mosey, flagged, harbicans, prepuces, kine, crone, upbraid*—and, if you want to know, I am still, or again, stuck with "mosey" and "barbicans." Then I reached "Agenbite of inwit," which I understood so well that I grew suspicious: surely it cannot mean THAT!

But it did.

There are a number of "barbicans" which I keep looking up and noting down, only to forget them again. Whenever I try to unmask them, I first note down what I think their true face is, before tracing them in the dictionary, and by this method I have arrived at a number of "solutions" which, in intention, surely must stem from those earlier alchemistic efforts in which I would divine the English equivalent to certain Dutch words.

Here's a short list of intuitive lexicography:

*propinquish*—propose in halting manner.
*barbican*—wooden appendix protruding from ceiling.
*obstreperous*—striped in obnoxious fashion.
*inchoate*—darkly unsuited.

*anodyne*—biting liquid used for facial cleansing after shaving incident.

*maverick*—unusual in old Balkan way.

*uxorious*—forcefully nagging.

*enjoined*—merged unknowingly.

*sedulous*—sable covered.

*spinnaker*—dizzy sailor.

*emunctory*—oozing orifice.

*arcane* (as in "arcane knowledge")—ancient lore, whispered beneath arches or under arc-lights.

Looking at this list, I am struck by a difference between Dutch and English which is never very apparent to English-speakers: the extent to which their language is *not* German—I mean Teutonic—I mean stemming from those dense forests between the North Sea coast in the west and, say, the outer reaches of Poland in the east, in the time before the Romans brought the tribes there to heel. In the above list, I think only "spinnaker" can be traced to the forests; the rest crossed the Channel with William the Conqueror, hailing ultimately from Rome and Greece. There is a funny difference between the way an Englishman uses words like *anthropology, psychology, democracy, orifice, noxious,* etc.—as if they are his own—and the way a Dutchman deals with his Graecisms and Latinisms, such as *democratie, extreem, theocratie, pieteit, psychologie, notaris, reparatie, bibliothecaris, secretaris, amfibie, mobiel, ornitholo-gie,* etc. In Dutch these are clearly funny birds, wholly unlike "schuur" (barn); but in English they have, for historical reasons, sunk deeper into common parlance, so that these Mediterranean borrowings are now being paraded as the only possible and at the same time wholly English word. For instance, "History" ("Historie" in Dutch). We have, in addition to the fob from down south, the real thing ("Geschiedenis") at our disposal, but a false sense of cosmopolitanism adheres to the English "History" and is supposedly lacking in the Dutch "Geschiedenis." I think that this kind of misconception may be an additional factor accounting for the silly veneration with which the English language is often approached in my country.

My first proper read in English was Russell's *History of Western Philosophy*. For much of 1969 I was doing the washing-up in the kitchen of an old castle in Devon—Dartington Hall—which once belonged to Henry the Eighth, and in which, amongst other things, a College of Art was established. It was an unlikely stop on the way to university, but there I found myself doing the dishes while my girlfriend was attending the dance & drama course. In my vain efforts to scale the rocky heights of philosophy, I had brought Karl Jaspers' book on Kant with me in Dutch translation. And it got me nowhere. I couldn't follow it and felt repulsed. I started to nurse rather grim feelings towards that impenetrable fortress of philosophy, within the walls of which I hoped people were studying man's ultimate questions, possibly even resolving them, but so far without letting me in.

I couldn't find an entrance anywhere and was about to go into a sulk when one day, in the family library at Dartington, I stumbled onto Russell's *History of Western Philosophy*. From the sombre citadel I had dreamt up, this sprightly man came trotting out to me, and with one wave of his hand dispelled all my sulks and misgivings. His boyish charm, his malicious humor, and above all his keen sharpness swept me along on an unforgettable journey through twenty-five centuries of Western thinking. He was such a delight to read because he personally went out into the field with, or against, the philosophers he described. I had never read anyone who was so impressively knowledgeable, authoritative, and funny at the same time. Some quotes: "Erasmus was incurably and unashamedly literary." On Machiavelli: "It is the custom to be shocked by him." On Spinoza: "Intellectually, some others have surpassed him, but ethically he is supreme. As a natural consequence, he was considered during his lifetime, and for a century after his death, a man of appalling wickedness." On Hume and Rousseau: "Rousseau was mad but influential, Hume was sane but had no followers."

Much later I learned that Russell's *History* sadly lapses when he gets to the nineteenth century, but that is not relevant here. For me, as I was at that time, lingering in half-sulk in front of that Venerable Temple of Western Wisdom, my greatest luck was to be greeted by Bertrand Russell at the entrance. He is a witty and brilliant host, and even if not all those at the party get the attention they deserve, his company was an overwhelming compensation. I still cherish my copy with the pencil portrait by Robin Guthrie on the jacket.

Up till then I had never encountered in Dutch a man who was so clever, learned, and amusing. I hate to say this, because I don't want to run my country down in any way, but I have to mention it here as stealthily as I can: there's an awful lot of intensely dull writing going on in Dutch academia, and it has been going on there for decades on end, and will go on for decades to come, this time in English, I'm afraid—almost a guarantee of drabness, in view of the local command of the venerated tongue.

In Holland you would, for instance, find it hard to encounter the likes of Gilbert Murray, J. B. Bury, Francis Cornford, Maurice Bowra, H. D. F. Kitto, Moses Finley, Benjamin Jowett, W. K. C. Guthrie—to mention only the names that readily come to my mind, with their brilliant commentaries and wonderful translations from classical history and philosophy. Reading Plato in Dutch in the sixties, I would have had to hack my way through a dense undergrowth of grammatically correct but hopelessly lifeless prose, emanating inevitably from the boring provincialism of the translators, and leaving the reader with the wrappings of a mummy. But reading Plato in English, I was immediately swept along. The insight, the clothes, the flirting, the markets, the courtyards, the personalities, the jokes—in English, the whole thing sprang to life inescapably. Plato's *Republic*, which I read in the summer of 1969, has forever remained one of my happiest encounters on paper.

I will not bore you with the ins and outs of the Dutch educational system. Be it said, however, that it lacks the possibility which was so gloriously rampant in the English public school system, of maintaining a broad and deep connection with the ancients. In Holland, and even more so, of course, in the intellectually humble milieu I stem from (I may be confusing the two), Plato was sadly entombed in the dusty glass cupboard of the Past.

By 1970 my familiarity with English had far outgrown anything I had ever achieved in German or French. In some areas, I even think that my English was better than my Dutch—mainly in matters intellectual. There was a stage where the intrusion went so far that whenever I dreamt about my family back in Holland, they spoke English to me and each other. I never thought the parrot could travel so deeply into a man's soul. My spoken English was virtually accentless then, though people with a keen ear did suspect I might have something to do with South Africa. (An accent I did not know at the time. When I did get to know it, I thought someone was having me on, because to a Dutchman a South African sounds like a Dutchman who is deliberately refusing to pick up the right accent—somewhat in the way the French and English often diligently abuse each other's parlance by wilfully contorting the other nation's speech.)

So I waded—or swam, rather—deeply into English, and read Kant, Schopenhauer, Nietzsche and, most important to me, Wittgenstein's *Tractatus* and *Philosophical Investigations* in English translation, though I could easily have handled these works (language-wise) in the original German. As a consequence, I made the common mistake of thinking about Wittgenstein as a British philosopher with a vague Viennese past, which accounted for his annual trip there around Christmas. This is, of course, a silly view of Wittgenstein, whom I later came to know as primarily a Viennese thinker, one who only halfheartedly took up his sojourn in Britain, as so many other Viennese were forced to do in the thirties, if they were Jewish.

Reading those German philosophers in English was a bit daft, as it misled me into a wrongheaded assessment of some aspects of their thinking. Luckily, quite the reverse happened when I read Proust in Scott Moncrieff's translation. I may have missed out on bits of the Germans in English, but I would have missed out on lots of Proust in Dutch, had there been a translation around at the time. There is quite an enormous societal overlap between late-nineteenth-century French and English ways of being artistic, a snob, a litterateur, a dandy, a Jockey Club member, a society hostess, a scion of a noble house, a maid-servant, or a hopelessly middle-class riser. All these are ways of being which certainly had their vague equivalents in our parts, but not with the added dash of being relevant in the international political and cultural arena of the time. I mean, you could take a coach from Wilde's Bedford Square to a soirée at the Duchesse de Guermantes'. No such clear connection existed between Amsterdam, on the one hand, and Paris and London, on the other. It is unimaginable for any Dutch author to be met in Amiens the way Ruskin was encountered there by Proust. This is not a reflection on Dutch authors of the period, but rather an expression of the international situation at the time. How many Lithuanian, Latvian, Finnish or Basque novelists are internationally coming to the fore at present?

In 1972, after having graduated in philosophy, I returned to Amsterdam to take up medicine. I had been away in England for almost five years, and soon after my arrival, to my utter dismay, I sat through the spectacle of a medical professor solemnly writing out in English, on the blackboard in the lecture theater, the reasons for which general practitioners refer patients to consultants in hospitals:

*because we do not know.*
*because we cannot do.*
*because we need support.*

—giving the final touch of imbecility by the gnarled way in which he pronounced these three simple phrases.

In Holland, and in many other parts of the world, the type of idolatry I was talking about earlier is one of the most repulsive effects of the fact that English is now lording it globally. In my own profession, there is a lamentable inclination to use English phrases when talking about matters that can be described perfectly well in our own language. What to think of a designation such as "the blue toe syndrome," used to refer to a patient with a circulatory problem? Doctors have dropped Latin but now seize on English phrases in which to wrap up the rather humdrum contents of many of their concepts. "Irritable bowel syndrome" is a standard diagnosis which can easily be phrased in Dutch, but then it loses that clinical polish which keeps the patient at bay. The doctor needs these fancy phrases to protect his domain.

Computer idiom is inevitably adapted—*download, boot start, surf, chat, online, mail, hard disk, update, delete, crash, e-mailing,* etc.—but the English is subsequently maltreated when the verbs are being conjugated. For "downloaded" you get "ge-download" (don't bother to pronounce it) or "downgeload." For "surfed," past tense, you obtain "surfte." "Deleted" becomes "ge-deleted," I guess. And "crashed" turns into "crashte." How would you like "downloadized" or "surfetted" or "croshed" or "be-mailed" or "chatten" as conjugations?

These are ugly results. Uglier still are the many academic Ph.D. theses written in Holland in English. I don't think it really matters when you are dealing with atoms, bridges, teeth, arteries, or gamma rays, but when you are writing about people and ought to throw in a little of your own personality in order to infuse some life into the thing, the handicap of having to do this in English is severely debilitating. People rarely realize this and therefore tend to use English as if it were a dead language, like Esperanto, with an equally lifeless outcome.

But ugliest of all are the scenes in which Dutchmen think they can speak English fluently, often lured on by repeated assurances of native speakers (who will say, "But your English is marvelous!" —a thing they wouldn't dream of saying to one of their countrymen). Thus I once witnessed, in agony, a colleague of mine being slaughtered on a BBC program. He had walked into the studio, in all innocence, for a frank but fair exchange on the (to him) crystal-clear subject of euthanasia. Ludovic Kennedy was there to help him out, Michael Ignatieff was in the chair, and the opposition consisted of Dame Ciceley Saunders—the Holy Virgin of the Hospice Movement—and two supercilious British neurologists who, talking down from incredible heights of arrogance, explained to my colleague that he was killing off his patients in his ignorance of proper medical treatment. Now, the poor man's English was not so bad that he couldn't say, "The coronary arteries are on the surface of the heart" or "My uncle Dick was a butcher," but to fight off these two, he needed really to speak the language, to live an emotion in words—words which now utterly failed him. Overwhelmed by righteous indignation but blocked by his lack of English, he was reduced to a spluttering heap. It was a horrible lesson about the emptiness of knowing a few words and phrases and about the fullness of a spoken language. There is a vast difference between showing someone the way to the railway station in English and showing him the way to Plato. This is often overlooked by city-map speakers.

Living in Holland, I encounter many people who speak a little English, mostly of too dull a variety to sharpen my own English on. So I only run into proper English on paper or on television or in the cinema. As a consequence, my passive English is still all right, but my active English barely keeps in shape, and I fear it is not getting any more vigorous.

Writing in English at first felt to me like trying to plough a stretch of marble: an ungainly procedure, ruining some pretty nice material, and the result was nil. I feel reasonably comfortable now writing in English—though please note that is something I would never say about writing in Dutch. Why not? Well, it's the difference between a natural biped (man) and a circus biped (dog). You wouldn't ever say to a human that you admire the way he manages so well on two legs, while a dog is applauded for just this feat. The dream of a foreign writer using English is that the natives will forget about his dogginess and say to each other: I just love the way he moves.

But, comfortable or not, I still have to shrug off a slight resentment at having to put on these funny clothes in order to be let in. I suppose that I could counter this by pitying you for missing out on certain Dutch authors whose virtues I couldn't begin to try to expound to you—no more than I could give someone an idea of Jimi Hendrix's guitar-playing by whistling a few notes. Though I wouldn't argue absolutely against this possibility, the fact is that I cannot do it right here.

There remain, however, many areas where I do not know my way around in English, and I am not only thinking of barbicans and obstreperous arcaneness, but terms of carpentry, for instance, or automobile parts, or shipping terms, or bird names. I will always confuse grebes, sparrows, thrushes, curlews, and snipes. I am, in English, strictly a pigeon–blackbird–duck man (but only ornithologically, he added hastily).

I am, to put it briefly, not a native speaker, and I don't mind.

# French Without Tears

## Luc Sante

My parents and I emigrated to the United States from the French-speaking part of Belgium when I was a child. The move was made for pressing economic reasons and was lamented by my parents from the start; only intermittently did they have the leisure and lightheartedness to plunge into the adventure of their new surroundings. My mother spoke no English at first; my father relied on a weak memory of the language from his secondary studies, and he tended to mix it up with the more vigorous strain of German in him, acquired from growing up in a town scant miles from the linguistic frontier. In America my parents had few French-speaking acquaintances. The isolation was hardest on my mother, who was uneducated (both my parents left school in their middle teens), came from a particularly restricted and provincial background, and stayed at home, while my father, more cosmopolitan by nature, at least had the opportunity to mix with Americans and immigrants from other countries during his working hours. My mother therefore seized upon any and all instances of French in American life. A French-derived surname spotted on a signboard could cheer her up for an hour; a drive with my parents would be punctuated by my mother happily reading aloud from the roadside: *Chez Pierre!*

*Maison de Beauté*! When I watched cartoons on Saturday mornings, the whole family would gather for Pepe le Pew, the Gallic skunk forever making romantic advances to horrified black and white cats: *L'amour, toujours l'amour . . .*

During my first year of school in America, my mother drilled me in French for an hour every day when I got home. That was shrewd of her; at first I was so discombobulated by the shift in languages between home and school that for an hour or so on either side I was effectively unlanguaged, nearly aphasic. The drills were as effective at getting me back to French as schoolyard peer pressure was in forcing English upon me in the morning. After a while I could slide between languages with relative ease, and when my mother and I returned to Belgium for sojourns lengthy enough that I was sent to school there, I engaged the curriculum as if I had never been away at all. Those trips, made when I was not quite eight and not quite nine, respectively, marked a significant shift in our lives. Previously, my parents had maintained the hope that our stay in America was to be temporary, but when my maternal grandparents sickened and died, which made those trips necessary, an important link was severed. My father's parents were already long dead, and there was not much immediate family left. We were on our own, and might as well stay where opportunities grew densest. This decision did not improve the morale of the household. Thereafter my parents would try to maintain a semblance of Belgium in our home, but the enthusiasm was gone, and the simulacrum shifted, steadily if invisibly, away from its model. In the same way, the family language was progressively mongrelized. While keeping the pronunciation and syntax of French it became *franglais.*

For me the French language very nearly became detached from its base, like so many of our household customs, which had lost their connection to any wider world and hovered in a vacuum, fetishes that might as well have been invented by my parents to keep me alienated from my peers. But I had a fortuitous link to the world of francophone children: my father's sister and her husband, small-town newsagents, subscribed me to my favorite Belgian comic magazine. I read *Spirou* every week for ten years, and through it subcutaneously absorbed not just the living language but also a sense of daily life in a Belgium that was then changing much more rapidly than my parents realized. The comic weeklies (the others were *Tintin* and *Pilote,* the latter published in France) had no American equivalent; they combined about a dozen serial comic strips, on double-page spreads, with a handful of single-page gags, along with games, contests, educational tidbits, and some prose fiction I never so much as glanced at. I didn't care much about stories; I cared passionately about graphic style, and this affected my reading—I disdained the ostensibly serious yarns, with their conventionally realist draftsmanship, in favor of the wildest and funniest drawings. The funny strips also happened to be the most unbridled in their use of language, reveling in the singular ability of French to generate wordplay, puns in particular.

French-speaking children are schooled in puns from the start. Of course, this could be said of speakers of English and maybe every other language as well—that's what riddles are for. For example, I date my true immersion in English from the moment I understood the humor of Q: When is a boy not a boy? A: When he turns into a store. But puns lie much thicker on the ground in French, in large part because the language is so much more rigorous and willfully delimited than the sprawling mass of English, an elegantly efficient two-stroke engine to the latter's uncontainable Rube Goldberg mechanism. French does not necessarily have fewer sounds than English, but the protocols governing their order and frequency make their appearances predictable—hence the profusion of sound-alike phrases and sentences, which fueled Surrealism and ensure the ongoing appeal of Freudian and post-Freudian ideas in the French-speaking world: *Les dents, la bouche. Laid dans la bouche. Les dents la bouchent. L'aidant la bouche.* Etc. These phrases, which sound exactly alike, respectively mean "the teeth, the mouth"; "ugly in the mouth"; "the teeth choke her"; "helping her chokes her." You don't need to have been psychoanalyzed by Jacques Lacan to see from these examples how language can assist thought in swiftly tunneling from the mundane to the taboo. Children are instinctively aware of this, even and perhaps especially if they are being raised Catholic and are thus trained in the finer points of repression.

The most internationally famous characters in *Spirou* were Les Schtroumpfs, known in the English-speaking world as the Smurfs, small blue elfin creatures who lived in a toadstool village. In their English-language animated appearances they could be cloyingly cute, but in French they were spared this fate by their language, marked by an incessant use of the (invented) word *schtroumpf,* employed as noun, verb, adverb, adjective, and interjection. Every reader, no matter how young, understood this usage without a gloss, because it parodied the French conversational trope of substituting catchalls such as *truc, chose,* and *machin* for words that cannot immediately be called to mind, in any grammatical position. What *schtroumpf* highlighted was the ability of such dummy words to suggest words prohibited from writing or speech, regardless of the fact that the actual words *schtroumpf* was substituting for were always clear from context. *Truc* or *chose* became neutral from exposure, but *schtroumpf* subliminally spoke to the unconscious; its surface strangeness could make it mean things that the child's mind does not yet know but can imagine with tantalizing vagueness.

Not all the wordplay was so freighted, of course. In the Astérix series (tales of a Mutt-and-Jeff pair of winged-helmeted first-century Gauls, serialized in *Pilote*), the characters' names were always elaborate puns that turned on their suffixes, -ix for the Gauls and -us for the enemy Romans (to pick two that don't require lengthy glosses, one of the former was Madamboevarix, one of the latter Volfgangamadéus). Deciphering such names— and puns of that sort were rife in all the funny strips—provided an agreeable gymnastic exercise, especially if it took a week or two of rolling the name around before it clicked open like a combination lock. Meanwhile, the adventures of Tintin, the boy reporter, a Belgian (and eventually international) institution since the 1920s, featured as a recurring character Captain Haddock, an alcoholic and irascible but good-hearted old sea dog. He was noted for his pratfalls, and even more for the streams of insults he would launch at villains, thieving wildlife, cars that splashed puddle water at him on the street, or small boys who had hit him in the head with a ball: *Accapareurs! Coloquintes! Ophicléides! Patapoufs! Cloportes! Anthropophages! Catachrèses! Moujiks! Rhizomes! Ectoplasmes! Anthropopithèques! Analphabètes! Cornichons! Va-nu-pieds! Saltimbanques! Moules à gaufres! Protozoaires!* (Monopolists, bitter apples, serpents [the musical instrument], fatsos, woodlice, cannibals, catachreses, muzhiks, rhizomes, ectoplasms, Anthropopitheci Erecti, illiterates, gherkins, ragamuffins, mountebanks, waffle irons, protozoa.) It was an explosion in the dictionary, *Finnegans Wake* on a matchbook cover, a fantastically liberating surge of pure unshackled language. The comics provided an important lesson: Language could be a medium of fun, and not just safe, approved fun, either, but wild, anarchic, disruptive fun. There was nothing lazy or slapdash about the comics' employment of words, though; that much was clear even to an eight-year-old. Therefore, the appendix to the lesson was that fun could best be achieved through a thorough grounding in ballistics and a heightened sense of precision.

The value of precision was something I had been learning all my life, perhaps subliminally, from my father. He had quit school at fourteen to go to work; his father had done likewise; his grandfather had been illiterate. Nevertheless, both my father and his father were great readers. There was always at least one crowded bookcase in our home, much of its contents having been brought with us across the ocean—he was not only a great reader, but a great rereader. The books were diverse, to my eye, ranging from somber hardbound volumes in slipcases to lurid paperbacks I imagined as containing all the secret lore of the tribe of adults. Looking at them today (I made a point of saving the library's core after my parents sold their house and, almost immediately thereafter, died), I realize that the great majority of the books were bestsellers, items prominently displayed in Belgian bookstores between the late 1940s and the late 1950s. The lurid paperbacks, in fact, were nearly all published by the pioneering firm Marabout, a French-language phenomenon equivalent to a downmarket Penguin, that happened to be headquartered in our otherwise not very literary home town.

My father's books, then, could have been found in many other middle-class Belgian households of the period, and today they profusely line the shelves of secondhand bookshops. Not only are there no rarities among them, but scarcely any would have been seen among the effects of Parisian tastemakers. Few of them would be considered literary; not many date from before the period in which they were acquired. They were, nevertheless, the result of discriminating selection, and what they all had in common was style. There was not just one style among them, since they included popular novels, popular history, travel narratives, war memoirs, and humorous vignettes, but all of them answered my father's requirements. He was a stickler for *le mot juste,* that very French, very positivistic idea that there is one, and only one, exact word capable of expressing a particular idea in a particular circumstance. Style for him was a matter of both precision and elegance, which were entwined in any case. His classics included La Fontaine's fables, Molière's comedies, Victor Hugo's poems, and the late-nineteenth-century plays of Edmond Rostand, especially *Cyrano de Bergerac.* All these he cited continually, sometimes because they fit the occasion, sometimes because he merely wanted to savor their music.

At some early point in my life he inculcated in me the very model of elegance, the end of *Cyrano.* The dying hero tells his friends that *quelque chose que sans un pli, sans une tache / J'emporte malgré vous* (something spotless and unwrinkled, that despite you I'm taking with me). He lifts high his sword, proclaims *et c'est* (and it is); the sword drops from his hand and he falls into the arms of his companions. Roxane kisses his forehead, asks *C'est?* Cyrano opens his eyes, recognizes her and says, smiling, *Mon panache.* Curtain. *Panache* literally means the plume of a hat, as worn by a seventeenth-century gentleman, but it also means what it does in English, only more so. Thus we have the pun in the last breath of life, the expression of wit as an exemplary act of heroism, the manifestation of a principle in the very utterance of its name. I was reminded of this years later when I learned that apprentice *toreros* call themselves "students of elegance," but if the Spaniards are equally capable of deeming elegance to reach its summit when it brushes against death, only the French could conceive of the matter as intrinsically verbal.

Elegance and precision are necessary allies; together they indicate the presence of truth. Nowhere is this axiom more clearly illustrated than in the fables of Jean de la Fontaine (1621–1695). Nearly every francophone can recite, at least, *tout flatteur vit aux dépens de celui qui l'écoute* (every flatterer lives at the expense of whoever listens to him), from the fable of the Crow and the Fox. I knew the tune before I knew the words, as it were—the phrase was burned into my mind before I could define the word *dépens* (expense), and although I had a fair idea of what the phrase meant, it was as much a mantra as a moral. By the time I was of age to understand all the implications of the phrase, I knew its music to be a further guarantee of its wisdom. So it was with a sense of deep familiarity that, when I was in my twenties and by then a working writer, I first read Flaubert's famous letter to George Sand:

> When I come upon a bad assonance or a repetition in my sentences, I'm sure I'm floundering in the false. By searching I find the proper expression, which was always the only one, and which is also harmonious. The word is never lacking when one

possesses the idea. Is there not, in this precise fitting of parts, something eternal, like a principle? If not, why should there be a relation between the right word and the musical word? Or why should the greatest compression of thought always result in a line of poetry?

My father never read Flaubert, and yet he had transmitted to me something of his essence—in part because some of Flaubert's ideas had existed in French literature long before he articulated them, and in part because some had been broadly disseminated since his time. By the time I read the letter, its message was already for me an article of faith.

Nevertheless I avoided my father's books, and to this day I've read very few. The obvious Freudian interpretation is probably not irrelevant, although more pedestrian reasons seem just as valid now as they did then. I was bored by the very idea of most of them: the mountaineering sagas of Frison-Roche, the broad peasant comedies of Arthur Masson, the orotund Catholic and patrician moral tales of Jean de la Varende. The only books I plucked from his shelves were the crime novels, by Simenon and others, which he hated and never read, but which his sister and her husband, who were wonderful people as well as newsagents but who regarded all books as indiscriminate product, sometimes threw into the parcels they sent our way. These and the comic magazines constituted the bulk of what was available for me to read in French in my youth. In English, though, I was trying as well as I could to cultivate precociously advanced tastes—I wanted to find literature as hip as the music I enjoyed. Another sort of gap between the languages was forming.

Then, when I was just the right age, we traveled to Montreal to take in Expo 67. It was the first time any of us had been in a French-speaking country in more than four years, and I was at least as excited by the prospect of visiting bookstores as by the fair itself. In my recollection, possibly telescoped by time, a center-city *librairie* was our very first stop. I don't know whether I had anything particular in mind before going in, but I came away with two books. One of them was André Breton's *Anthologie de l'humour noir,* an excellent choice if one made by happenstance—"black humor," a literary genre spawned by Lenny Bruce as much as anybody, was all the rage in the U.S. then, and that's what I thought I was getting. The other was a fat paperback anthology of French poetry, published by Marabout. I wasn't very much interested in poetry, except maybe stray bits of Beat stuff I'd seen here and there, but in flipping through the volume I noticed that many of the poems looked different from what I'd generally been exposed to: some had very long lines, some were studded with proper nouns, some were even in prose, if such a thing was possible. That night I lay on my bed in the motel room in Longueil and opened the book to

*A la fin tu est las de ce monde ancien*

"In the end you are tired of this old world." Thus began "Zone," by Guillaume Apollinaire.

*Bergère ô tour Eiffel le troupeau des ponts bêle ce matin.* "Shepherdess o Eiffel Tower the flock of bridges is bleating this morning." The poem was speaking directly to me, to me alone, as proven on the second page: *Voilà la jeune rue et tu n'es encore qu'un petit enfant / Ta mère ne t'habille que de bleu et de blanc.* "Here is the young street and you are but a little child / Your mother only dresses you in blue and white," which was exactly true of my early childhood; that *tu* clinched it. *Tu regardes les yeux pleins de larmes ces pauvres émigrants / Ils croient en Dieu ils prient les femmes allaitent des enfants / Ils emplissent de leur odeure le hall de la gare Saint-Lazare.* "You look with your eyes filled with tears at the poor immigrants / They believe in God they pray the women suckle infants / They fill with their odor the hall of the Saint-Lazare station"—I had been there and seen that! Furthermore, the poem seemed to be about a yearning for modernity in the face of confusion as to the truth of religion, a clairvoyant depiction of my own central inner drama of the time. But there was more: the poem was fluid, rhyming but in an elastic meter like an improvised song, with phrases strung together without punctuation but always clear in their meaning, with an unlabored syntax close to conversational, with capitalized names like cherries in a box of chocolates, with sudden movements in time and space executed with a casual legerdemain, with a flash and whirl and continual surprise that was just what I wanted from the modern world but with a palpable kindness that reassured me as the poem flung me about.

At that moment I became a French modernist, and I suppose I've never stopped being one, despite appearances. French was capable of astounding feats unavailable to most languages, it seemed to me. In his poem *"L'union libre,"* one of the most erotic works in all literature, André Breton wrote: *Ma femme à la bouche de cocarde et de bouquet d'étoiles de dernière grandeur / Aux dents d'empreintes de souris blanche sur la terre blanche / À la langue d'ambre et de verre frottés / Ma femme à la langue d'hostie poignardée.* What does it give in English? "My woman with her cockade mouth, the mouth of a bouquet of stars of the greatest magnitude / With teeth of the footprints of a white mouse on the white earth / With her tongue of polished amber and glass / My woman with her tongue of a stabbed host." It's not terrible, maybe, but it has none of the music or the magic, in part because of the tendency of English to condensation and bluntness, away from the silken chains of prepositional phrases that give French its incantatory power. Of course, languages are never equivalent, can never be measured on the same scale, but when French lyricism is translated into English, the English version always sounds lead-footed, boorish, resolutely unsexy. Take the phrase *hostie poignardée*—the profanation of the transubstantiated body of Christ in the form of a white disk of bread. The French phrase enacts the violence onomatopoeically, following the serene *hostie* with the triple puncture of *poignardée,* and you even see the dagger, the *poignard.* In English, "stabbed host," pretty much the only way of expressing the thought in less than a sentence, suggests a murder-robbery in a highway diner as reported over a police radio, while musically it is a coarse cluster of dentals, and it is over in a second and leaves no echo.

The French language opened poetry to me, and I wrote as well as read it throughout my teens, albeit in English since I did not trust my command of the nuances of French. Eventually I came to love English-language poetry as well, but never quite in the same way. Had I been stopped on the street and ordered to recite a line of poetry, I would automatically have said: *J'ai tendu des cordes de clocher à clocher; des guirlandes de fenêtre à fenêtre; des chaînes d'or d'étoile à étoile, et je danse* ("I stretched ropes from spire to spire, garlands from window to window, gold chains from star to star, and I dance"—Rimbaud).

Midway through college, I stopped writing poetry altogether. I doubted my talent, but I also had found what I thought was the authentic music of the American language, in the prose of Dashiell Hammett, Raymond Chandler, and James M. Cain. "They threw me off the hay truck about noon," the opening sentence of *The Postman Always Rings Twice,* seemed to exemplify in nine words all the highest virtues of American prose. It was plain, unadorned demotic speech, resolutely laconic and flat, containing a whole landscape of gas stations and bus depots and bars, of dollar bills and cigarette butts and spit, stuff I had encountered in daily life that seemed to stare down literature and dare it to cross the line in the dirt. It defied all the verities and aesthetics of the university in which I was a half-reluctant conscript, of course, but no less significant was the fact that it embodied the inverse of everything I thought I knew about French.

The importance of both causes was emphasized by the fact that my epiphany occurred in Paris, where I was attending a summer program sponsored by my college that was devoted to the very latest manifestations of French critical thought. What was I doing there? The previous year I had signed up for a course given in the French department on Surrealism, a subject of enduring interest to me. Not ten minutes into the first class I was at sea. The instructor, a recent Parisian transplant, drew cryptic diagrams on the blackboard while issuing a rapid-fire stream of references, quotes, unfamiliar Greek-derived words, and puns. The latter, at least, I could appreciate, although they were unfunny and often ponderous (an English-language one, "French Freud," was to reappear continually as a catch-phrase), and were redolent of forced play; it was like watching academics dance at a disco in order to make a point. As a chronic shirker of math requirements, I was dismayed by the diagrams and the scientific or pseudo-scientific tone of the propositions; I had never heard of Lacan or Derrida; and what did any of it have to do with Surrealism? It seemed to me the equivalent of getting to know someone by administering chloroform and then dissecting her or him on a slab. Somehow I completed the year, and achieved a grade that did not disgrace me. I can only imagine that I signed up for the summer program because it would get me to Paris with an educational alibi. Somehow I even managed to obtain financial aid for the adventure.

The courses were a mixed lot. The art historian was genuinely riveting, although I remember more vividly the specialist in modern fiction, who seemed to devote the entirety of his analysis of *Madame Bovary* to rolling names and phrases around in his mouth until they became puns by force of will, for instance mangling "Charles Bovary" until it yielded up *charivari*. Finally I was sick of puns, sick of the alleged *jouissance* of language, very nearly sick of French itself, and I hiked up to Galignani, the venerable English bookshop on the Rue de Rivoli, and picked up American books primarily composed of words of one syllable. But when I look at my notebooks from that time I am forced to acknowledge that every choice I made was saturated by the French spirit, the version prevailing at the time in particular. My approach to American crime fiction was that of an outsider, was informed by the *Série Noire* collection, by the ideas on American movies held by the critics at *Cahiers du Cinéma,* by Sartre's enthusiasm for the work of Faulkner, which he said resembled the view out the back window of a moving car. Despite myself I was in love with the chic that imbued all manifestations of the

French intellect. I was seduced by the French tendency to wrench words and phrases and even entire narratives from all context the better to prize them as artifacts, the way oily rags become art when framed with a broad white mat. I was enthralled and frustrated in equal measure by the French literature of the time that seemed intended for admiration rather than actual reading, dependent for its effect on a title, or an allusion to something classical and recondite, or a typographical decision, such as a thin scatter of fragments around the page like so many notes on a refrigerator door, or a block of unparagraphed and perhaps unpunctuated prose running on for the entirety of a slim volume.

Not long after my return I lost contact with the French-speaking world once again. This was to prove a pattern, with French waxing and waning in my life at long intervals, like the moon of a large planet. I did not set foot in my native land for another fifteen years, and then for a decade I went there annually, ostensibly to do research for a book. I made friends; I acquired a neighborhood and a set of site-specific habits; I got so that I could regain my fluency in the language within 24 hours of deplaning. It was then that I discovered several other kinds of French. The language that appeared in the media, in advertisements, and in the mouths of the more urban and well-connected people I met was quite different both from the tongue I had learned as a child and that which appeared in the books I read. It was bright and cold and hard-edged, implied technology and market research and modern accounting practices. I knew that it had its American parallel, which I generally avoided and often mocked, but I took this kind of French personally, like a slap. When some of its words leaked into my conversation because I had no friendly synonyms at hand in which to express a particular thought, it felt like an unhealthy imposture, as if I had caught myself putting on a gold tie—I suppose I felt like a class traitor, antiquated notion though that may be. Even unarguable statements made using those words felt like lies, since the language so clearly had been produced in a laboratory.

But I also immersed myself in argot, *la langue verte* (the green tongue). I had encountered it before, notably in my mid-twenties, when I hung out on both continents with a group of radical offspring of French academic families who affected *verlan* (backslang, then just on the cusp of becoming chic) and conducted entire conversations in prison slang without glossing anything for my benefit, making me feel excluded and desperately unhip. But by a decade or two later the lingo had penetrated more deeply into the everyday speech of ordinary folk, and I absorbed a good deal of it from reading, in particular from crime novels of the 1950s and '60s. American slang, whatever its origin, tends to fill particular lexical slots, usually pertaining to highly charged categories of meaning—sex and drugs and crime in particular. French slang is even more rooted in crime, but it is defiant rather than furtive. It is an entire language, a parallel verbal world that mocks the formal protocols of the master language. Unlike the American variety, it contains words for every sort of thing, for "door" and "table" and "cup." Some of it is ancient, dating back to the time of François Villon and beyond; some of it actually derives from Romany, and it continues to loot other languages, in pointed contrast to official French, which proscribes loan-words. It is a highly metaphorical language, as slang tends to be, with an insolent, blaring music and a staccato beat: *Quand le bruit se répand que la poule tape aux fafs dans un coin, vous voyez les tapis se vider de tous les tricards.* Literally, this would more or less mean: "When the noise spreads that the hen is tapping for papers in a corner, you see the carpets emptying themselves of all the tricksters." What it signifies is: "When word gets around that the cops are checking IDs in the neighborhood, all the parolees instantly vanish from the bars." I derive deep satisfaction and sensual pleasure from argot, as little as I use it in the course of things. It is almost as if French and American had mated in the night and produced another tongue with all of the advantages of both, and none of the pomposities.

French was once the international language of diplomacy but is no more. It barely hangs on to its association with the courtly arts. It has been forced into retreat, in one domain after another, before the Anglo-Saxon juggernaut. This diminished status has occasioned both a resentful provincialism and the unfortunate tongue of technocrats and *biznessmen*. Its literature is rarely and haphazardly translated into English these days. The romance of French among poetically inclined American youths has waned considerably, in part because of the very success of French theory and its particular brand of double dutch, the nuances of which sometimes require a profound knowledge of classic literature, although this is not always apparent to English speakers. Where I live, in rural America, it is an obscure joke. It is my mother tongue, although I will probably seldom encounter again the specific variety of it I heard while growing up, since it was the instrument of a class that has changed drastically and to which I have lost most of my connections. I don't even employ it every week, let alone every day, and yet one way or another it informs every decision I make in the screen language I employ in order to pass unmolested in the land where I have lived for most of my life without ever shedding my internal foreignness. French is my secret identity, inaccessible to my friends. Sometimes I feel as though I have it all to myself.

# *Prelude*

## Thomas Laqueur

I seem to have had a peculiar loyalty to the German language from about as early as a child can articulate views. I was told by my parents that when they urged me as a three-year-old to learn Turkish, so that I might communicate more effectively with my playmates in Istanbul, where they had come in their flight from Hitler, I would have nothing of it. Let them learn German, I supposedly said; Turkish "ist eine hässliche Sprache." My feelings about speaking German, and more generally about being European, have become stronger as what few real connections I had ever had to the language, to Germany, or to Europe have all but disappeared.

German was my mother tongue. I mean this partly in the usual sense—my first language was German. But it is also true that I spoke it almost entirely with my mother, my grandmother and their women friends. Only certain words and phrases are spoken by men or to men in my linguistic fantasy life. German is almost entirely a self-contained family language for me, but it is also the language of a world—real, remembered, and misremembered— that my parents lost, a world that now exists almost entirely in my imagination, but which I maintain as a way of mourning them and theirs.

I spoke only German until we left Turkey in November 1949. A stop in London with relatives was still all German, as were a brief few weeks in New York. My mother's brother—my Onkel Otto—and his wife lived in Manhattan near Fort Tryon Park, in the middle of a German-Jewish ghetto. Later, when we had settled in West Virginia, my mother visited them periodically and came back complaining about how insular their world was. I think I understand what she meant: one could not forget that one was living in exile there, amidst one's countrymen on the cliffs above the Hudson. In contrast, my family's relationship to its native language could not have been more cut off from its roots than ours was in the coal villages and towns where I grew up. I do not think my parents thought of themselves as living in a diaspora because they had no one with whom to share their loss.

After New York, we lived for a few months in my father's sister's boarding house near the University of Texas. She specialized in housing foreign students. My Tante Eli and her husband had gone to Yugoslavia when Hitler came to power. When Hitler attacked Belgrade, they made their way south from Dubrovnik and Mosta to Albania, in the hope of being captured by the possibly benign Italians instead of by the certainly murderous Germans. They succeeded, and spent the war until 1942 in a Calabrian internment camp; then they were liberated by the British Eighth Army and headed north with it as translators. By the time they had to earn a living in Texas, they had Italian and Yugoslav and colloquial English in addition to very good school French—and Latin, in case an ancient Roman turned up. This was my first sustained exposure to English.

I remember being grumpy about learning a new language while in Austin. I do not remember saying what my parents claimed were my first words in my new language: "me no eat fruit." I find this unlikely, given that I have no memory of ever not liking any fruit, but still, this is family lore.

After three months of crowded living, my mother, paternal grandmother, younger brother and I joined my father in a hollow near Montgomery, West Virginia, where he had secured a job as a pathologist in a private coal-field hospital. A friend from Istanbul, also a pathologist, had found a job near there the year before, through a Jewish relief agency. I have no memory of speaking English during our months in that hollow, just up from a railroad track. I think my mother's English was not very good, so we didn't see much of the neighbors. Tante Biba and Onkel Peter, the friends from Istanbul, lived twenty or thirty miles away, and with them I of course spoke German. Then on to Bluefield, the "air-conditioned city," where coal poured in from the southern West Virginia bituminous coal-fields to one of the Norfolk and Western Railroad's biggest train yards. It was here that I started to learn English seriously. I remember no hostility this time, although I do remember being teased about my German accent for many years to come. Unlike my brother, who is three years younger than I am, I never acquired the mountain accent, and I still sound foreign in those parts.

It was in Bluefield that I discovered German was a language that people other than my parents and a few friends actually spoke. It was not, as I had unselfconsciously assumed, a family code. This revelation came as follows: I was having a screaming fight in German with my brother, in front of the Pen Mar Grocery, a half-block from our house on North Street; he was three and I six. The issue was how much of a two-barrel popsicle I was going to share with him. A lady came up to us and said, in German, that she would give us a nickel so that each of us could have a treat of our own. I do not remember buying a second popsicle, but I do remember being very excited at finding someone else of our linguistic species. I rushed home with the big news.

Frau Bressler, as she was called, had asked where we lived; I had told her. She visited. Frau Bressler had married Herr Bressler, who was many years her senior, after a long courtship. He had some sort of a disease that had caused his hands to shrivel into reddish, claw-like appendages, and he worked repairing small electrical appliances and meters. The Bresslers were poor; she was a southern German Catholic. (This I deduced on a visit last summer, from books about a papal visit to Bavaria I saw on the coffee table of her house.) Frau Bressler became one of my mother's close friends despite their very different circumstances. She also became our regular—indeed only—babysitter when my parents were away for more than an evening.

There was a third German in Bluefield, Frau Snelling, who had married—after the war, I assume—an alcoholic West Virginia forester. I associate her, however, not with making German a more public language for me, but rather with my first note-worthy failure in my efforts to be a good little German boy. The traumatic moment came when her mother, Frau Wöppekind, visited from Germany. I did, on meeting her, remember to address her with the formal *Sie,* as I had been told to do. I did not, however, remember to bow. "Mach eine Verbeugung," said my mother, not pleased with my lapse. I do not recall what Frau Wöppekind said, but I do remember that she seemed manifestly taken aback by "der Bube's" ill manners.

So now there were three strangers who spoke German in my world. I knew they were strangers because I addressed them as Frau or Herr instead of Onkel or Tante, which is what I called almost all other German-speaking adults. The fact that, following local custom, I called American adults who were close friends by their first names made our linguistic isolation palpable. Eddie and Janie and C.O. and Hazel were simply from another universe, where other laws pertained. I was in my late twenties before I could comfortably address grown-up Europeans by their first names, and even then it was not easy. The crisis came when I got a job at Berkeley and was placed on a committee with two older colleagues: Paul Alexander, a saintly, extravagantly learned Byzantinist who was on the fringe of my family circle (the best friend of a cousin by marriage), and Nicholas Riasanovsky, a famous Russian historian. We were to give out money for graduate research projects. I could not call Alexander "Onkel Paul," as I might otherwise have done; "Onkel Nick" was of course out of the question. And I could not address colleagues as "Professor." So "Paul" and "Nick" it was, but not without a mental gulp. I still find this blurring of boundaries difficult.

There were two exceptions to this first-name rule: my mother's closest friends from Istanbul. Both were known by their nicknames. One, still alive, is "Dicke" or "die Dicke" ("the fat one"), who was supposedly once fat; the other was "Schweinchen" ("piglet"), whose nickname is a corruption of her maiden name, Schwerine. Schweinchen was sometimes Tante Paula; Dicke was always Dicke.

German, in other words, constituted a world that I knew intimately but also not at all. I had, growing up, only the vaguest sense that people outside our family circle actually lived and functioned in our private language. Although I spoke it fluently,

I got things having to do with the public/private distinction seriously wrong. The *du/Sie* question was never easy. In our family, of course, I used the familiar; likewise with family friends. I could use *Sie,* but it did not come naturally. I had to be coached and reminded, a formula for screwing up, a sign not so much of bad character but cultural cluelessness. Dicke's husband, Wiegand, was said to be *vornehm* ("refined," "high class"). I do not know on what this view was based, but when he visited it was said to be important that I, age seven, not *dutzt* him. I think I succeeded. But there were embarrassing lapses. When I was eleven or twelve, we visited Boston and made a pilgrimage to the butcher shop of Herr Thyssen, who was my parents' long-distance purveyor of German food. It came every few weeks to Beckley and Bluefield, packed on dry ice, via Greyhound bus: *Kaiserjadgwurst, Leberwurst, Blutwurst,* and other wursts I can only say and not spell; *stinkerkäse* (my name for Limburger cheese); every kind of dark bread. At Herr Thyssen's shop, introductions were made and I lapsed into *du;* he was clearly taken aback; my mother was appalled. There was nothing to do but try to disappear.

The same problem came up in regard to tone of voice and distance from one's interlocutor. I seemed to have always been off. "Mami" Putschar, the German-speaking wife of a Hungarian pathologist in Charleston whom we visited occasionally, always said to me that I sounded like a *Feldwebel.* Frankly I did not know what this was (it is a sergeant), because it is not the sort of word that comes up in family life; I did not play soldiers with anyone who knew the language. But it was clear that this was not a good way to sound. In college, where—in the persons of émigré professors—I met my first "stranger Germans," I knew that I was somehow standing too close to them when I spoke. It took time to get the right range.

My family's and my German was entirely cut off from Germany and from everything that had happened to the language since the 1930s. (The one exception was a pilgrimage to New York when I was in high school, to see the Brucke theater do Schiller's *Don Carlos*. This was the first and I think only German play my parents saw after the mid-1930s.) There were lots of German speakers in my life, but none had had any connections with the real sources of the language for decades. They were an odd assortment of émigrés, some native speakers, others part of the German cultural penumbra. In Beckley, where we had moved in 1956, there was only a Ukrainian orthodox couple who spoke German. He had studied medicine in Germany after escaping from the east; she was a self-consciously romantic sort who spoke a hyperbolic, soulful, Russian-accented version of my mother tongue. During the summers there were also my uncles and aunts, who came to visit our cottage by a lake in southwestern Virginia; there were my mother's buddies from Istanbul, and some even from her late twenties and early thirties in Germany; there was, early on, my grandmother's sister-in-law, who spoke a Polish-accented German; there were several Hungarians, including a voice teacher from Juilliard who had the deepest voice of anyone I knew; there was an Austrian nurse who had somehow linked up with a West Virginia dermatologist named Locksley, who spouted Shakespeare at the slightest provocation. And there were Max and his wife, who owned a bakery in the small town of Pulaski, Virginia, near our lake; both had tattoos on their arms from Auschwitz. Why they wanted to speak German with my mother is unclear. I did not wonder about it at the time. They also spoke Yiddish with my Onkel Otto when he visited. In any case, this was an eccentric linguistic universe.

I dwell on all of these childhood memories because German is for me the language of memory and loss, a linguistic *Prelude.* My German is, first of all, a connection with a pre-Oedipal me. I have never made love in German; I know no slang words for matters sexual, and few slang words of any sort. I would not know what it would mean to feel sexual in German. The gigantic impact of linguistic adolescence—when one comes to own one's language as a separate person, when it becomes something belonging to one's generation—is lost on me. My German is frozen, amber-like, not only in pre-war history but in childhood; with some few exceptions, it is emotionally fixed. The word for carraway seed, *kümmel,* is an adjective for a kind of bread on which one eats corned beef or chopped liver, i.e. rye bread; for me it describes a man who terrified me as a small child, *der kümmel Mann,* a beggar with a pox-marked face who stood outside our Istanbul apartment. Too little has happened to me in German to make the regular public uses of words mean what they should.

Powerful German words generally feel like they come from my mother; phrases, dicta, from my dad. *Sanft*—"soft" or "gentle"— I associate with her, although the phrase in which it comes back to me in the first instance is not hers. In my mind's ear it is from Schiller's "Ode to Joy"— . . . *Wo dein sanfter Flügel weilt* ("where your gentle wing may come to rest"). I think of the word in connection with my birthdays. On the evening of September 6th, from as early as I can remember until I was ten or so, my father and I would lie on a couch, I enfolded in his arms, and listen to a recording of Beethoven's Ninth. For the first years in West Virginia, it was the old 78s of the Furtwängler recording that would clack-clack-clack down until the whole stack had to be turned. Sometime around second grade, we switched to the Toscanini "long play" version that, miraculously, played for twenty-five minutes without a clack and went by, in its wild tempos, considerably faster than Furtwängler's more Germanic version. The ritual, however, did not change with conductors: lights were dimmed; during *die Neunte* there would be no talking or interruptions by other family members; we were alone. I wonder how, before record-players, Germans of my parents' class and generation learned their reverence for *die Neunte* ("the Ninth")— which, without further modification, can only mean Beethoven's. In German, or at least my parents' German, one puts just a little bit more emphasis on the article *die* and lingers just an instant on the noun *Neunte* than one would in a phrase like "the ninth symphony of Schubert" or "the ninth symphony of Mahler." I know that this work still has considerable cultural clout in Germany, or at least did until recently; the great national work of the nineteenth century, it was what Bernstein conducted at the fallen Berlin Wall. But I have no sense whether men and women of my generation would say the words like my parents did and feel what I learned to feel. Like so much German, I know these two words of the language almost entirely in isolation from all but friends and family.

*Geboren*—the adjective "born"—is a mother word. She, and only she, and no one since she died, would address me on my birthday with the redundant silliness of *mein einziger Erstgeborener* ("my only firstborn"). The suffix *-lein* that produces the diminutive in German is also my mother's: my father might occasionally have addressed me as Thomaslein—I do not remember— but my mother always did. Tommy, which is what they called me

93

in West Virginia, has always sounded silly to me; Tom is just a name; Thomaslein is very sweet. *Traurig* ("sorrowful") is a mother word, although I think my mother was in fact far happier than my father. She could not keep a tune for more than two measures but loved to sing a song called "Die Lorelei," the lyrics of which were by her favorite poet, Heinrich Heine. I have her copy of his complete poems that she kept on her night table and read most days of her life.

> *Ich weiß nicht, was soll es bedeuten,*
> *Daß ich so traurig bin,*
> *Ein Märchen aus uralten Zeiten,*
> *Das kommt mir nicht aus dem Sinn.*

"I do not know what it means, that I am so sorrowful; I cannot get out of my head a tale of the most ancient of times." This is roughly how I feel about things German in general: a "Märchen" fairy-tale built of projections and fantasies and memories that I cannot erase and that leave me melancholy.

In my family, we spoke German at the dinner table until I left for college because my grandmother claimed that she neither spoke nor understood English. This was clearly false—she read English papers and watched English TV—but feigning ignorance allowed her to maintain the fiction of otherworldly incompetence that she seems to have cultivated all her life and that kept her entirely out of public view. She did not venture outside family circles during her twenty-three years in America. My grandmother was born in 1873, in the waning of the Biederman era, the youngest daughter of six children. She went to school long enough to learn French; she played piano well; she and my grandfather lived for music, which they played four hands. They had heard Brahms conduct, early in their lives together, as well as many of the other great German conductors of the nineteenth century. (I know all this from their concert diary, which I inherited when my father died.) My grandmother could do all sorts of needlework. But she could not—or at least did not, in anyone's memory—so much as boil an egg. She stayed in Germany until December 1939 on the grounds that she did not want to leave her Bechstein grand piano. In America, she dressed and acted like a lady of a distant century, seemingly unaware that the world around her had changed. (She did read about the deaths of her contemporaries in the Aufbau, and remained alert until the ninety-fifth of her one hundred years.) The first of my fantasy Germanies is hers. The words I associate with her are *Es geht rapide bergab*—"things are going rapidly downhill"—something she said about herself from when she was in her late seventies to when she went gaga in her late nineties.

With my mother I spoke German exclusively until she died; I have not spoken it regularly since 1992. With my father I spoke only English, the grown-up language, the language in which I talked of science and medicine and politics. He did, in fact, speak English much better than my mother, but it was only much later, when I heard him on a Dictaphone machine summarizing an autopsy, that I realized how heavily accented his English was, almost parodically so.

There were, as I said, exceptions to this linguistic segregation. The few bits of really grown-up German I know, and the minimal sense I have of the rhythms of the language, are from sayings or maxims, *Sprichwörter,* that come from my father. (I wish I could rattle off those wonderful torrents of dependent clauses

and finish up with the verb, as grown-up German speakers do.)
Likewise curses come through him. *Mit der Dummheit kämfen
Götter selbst vergebens* ("With stupidity the gods themselves
fight in vain") was a big one, as was Kant's categorical imperative, which was recited with a special tone of reverence. I loved
its sounds and the fact that there was only one such rule, even if
it took a while to understand what it meant: *handle nur nach
derjenigen Maxime, durch die du zugleich wollen kannst, daß sie
ein allgemeines Gesetz werde* ("act only on that maxim by which
you can at the same time will that it should become a universal
law," which I understood in the still grander form, "act as if the
maxim of your action were to become through your will a universal law of nature").

*Donnerwetter* ("thunder weather") was the prelude to an
explosion of my father's anger and was often followed by *noch
ein mal* ("once again"). This malediction was frequently associ-
ated with the threat that if we continued to misbehave my mother
would call my father, who would then say *ein machtwort*—
literally, a "word of power," but really more like the definitive
warning of the super-ego. Since one of the other big sayings in
my family was *Quod licet Jovi, non licet bovi* (Latin sayings had
the authority of German ones), which meant "What is allowed to
Jupiter is not allowed to the ox," the "thunder weather / words of
power" combo carried a certain mythological terror. The Latin
saying itself was used mostly to explain why my reading of the
categorical imperative was mistaken in holding that the maxim
for some action of my father's included him. So, if it was okay for
him to be late when we all knew that lateness was indefensible
as a universal principle, the old *Jovi* exception was adduced. I
thought that this was fudging on the universality principle but
got nowhere with this line of argument.

The only curses I know are my father's, and they are ridiculously quaint. He would reproach my mother with *Was glaubst du das ich bin, ein Dukatenscheisser* ("What do you think I am? Someone who shits ducats?") every month as he was paying the bills. He was terribly anxious about money, having no one to back him up if he failed, but he must have known full well that his wife was frugal and extremely efficient at household management. *Lech mich am arse* (kiss my ass) was another, always attributed to Schiller's Götz von Berlichen. I have never used any of these phrases in public because I have no idea whether they mean anything in the outside world.

Two words belong to both parents and have universal resonance for me: *Unsinn* and *vernünftig*. Again, I do not know whether other German-speakers my age feel this way about them; for all I know, they resonate as they do for me only in my private language. *Unsinn* ("nonsense," "absurdity") had many applications and was often used as an expletive. But it is one of the few words from childhood that carried over into adolescence. *Mache keinen Unsinn* ("Don't do anything stupid") was the standard caution before my going out on a date. It did not apply to my driving, which was impeccable, but to "parking" on one of the hundreds of miles of strip mine roads around where we lived and necking the evening away. (There was nothing else to do in Beckley, but this nonsense had other things to recommend it.) *Unsinn* and *sei vernünftig* ("act reasonably") are the only German words that have any personal association with sex for me. They have other meanings, of course. Being *vernünftig* meant being governed by reason in all matters and applied to life generally, but in the absence of any other post-pubescent words, they still have a peculiar ring of sexual danger.

Although, as I said, I spoke English with my father, my sense of German as a language of loss comes through him. I felt strongly as I was growing up that he simply did not get what it meant to live in another culture. My mother, whose English was wildly ungrammatical and full of Germanic neologisms, got on well with the locals. She made a joke of misunderstanding, as when on her citizenship examination she answered that *ja, ja,* she "had been and was still a member of the Communist Party." She had been told by friends that if she did not understand a question—she often missed what people said if they spoke quickly or with especially pronounced mountain accents— she should simply answer "yes." Beckley and Bluefield abounded with Toni Laqueur malapropisms. But she fit in. My father was clueless. He somehow translated my high school graduation as *Abitur,* an occasion for much ceremony and for a punch bowl of Champagne and liquor-soaked fruit. This did not go over well with my high school friends. He tried at my parents' New Year's Eve parties to have everyone wear tuxedos and listen to Beethoven's Ninth. This also did not find wide acceptance.

And he seemed to have no sense of what his own past meant after Hitler. We had a recording of German university student drinking songs that we played often. He knew all of them; I even knew them. He had a picture of himself and his university fraternity brothers wearing their uniforms and displaying sabers. He had a small dueling scar above his hair line. None of this struck him as odd or ironic. Perhaps this is just an instance of the strategy my parents shared, attempting to mitigate the pain of having lost their homeland by neither assimilating nor living in a diaspora community, among others who had been displaced. They lived as much as they could in a bubble, eating food and speaking a language and listening to music that no one around them appreciated or understood. My German has inherited something of their cultural autarchy.

I do not want to suggest that I speak a childish German, or that I cannot get by doing adult things in the language. But whenever I do something grown-up in German, I am self-conscious about doing it; I am aware of the temporal chasm between now and then ("then" being the lives of my parents and my own childhood). My father never went back to Germany; my mother went back once, in 1955, to visit an old friend who had returned. She lucked upon Central Casting's nightmare of a taxi driver, who went on about all the good things the Nazis had done and how Americans misunderstood *die Hitlerzeit*. Never again. So both of them remained passionately German, but without any real contact with Germany. They drank only German wines. They staged an elaborate German Christmas complete with candles on the tree (until neighbors told them that American trees, cut a month in advance, would go up in flames). They listened almost exclusively to German music—*Parsifal* was on for Easter. They thought that the French were wrong to occupy the Rhineland in 1920, and wrongheaded about much else besides. So I lived a childhood produced by the children of nineteenth-century Jews, who imagined the land of Goethe and Schiller with little of its reality or recent history.

I went to Germany for the first time in 1992, when I was forty-seven. I was there as a tourist and spoke of little but rooms, food, and schedules. The first time I actually said anything in German that was neither about travel nor about the sorts of things one talks about in families—that is, the first time I felt that German was for me a public language—was in the summer of 1995 at a conference in Frankfurt. I asked a question in German of a journalist; he understood and answered; I asked a follow-up. I translated in whispers the lectures of colleagues for my wife, and found that I was good at it. On subsequent trips I have given my own lectures in German, sometimes at the request of my hosts but sometimes just because I wanted very much to reclaim the language for my parents.

I love being in Germany among my friends; it is a return to a place and a language and a cultural tradition that my parents never ceased to mourn. The people I know there are to a person cultivated, intelligent, liberal and welcoming. But I have no illusions about the phantasmic—arguably delusional—attachment I have to place and language. In 1995, my wife and I visited my mother's hometown, Holzminden an der Weser, a small city of about 30,000 not far from Hanover. It is in what was the heartland of Nazi electoral strength. My grandparents' house looked exactly as it did in pictures, almost entirely unchanged. The river Weser ran swiftly less than a hundred meters from the little meadow where my grandfather, a grain merchant, kept a few cows and chickens.

I knocked on the door of the house, and an old woman appeared at the window. I asked her if she had lived here for a long time. Yes, she had always lived there. Well, I said, my grandparents had once lived there. No, not possible, she said before she relented: who were they? Their name was Weinberg. *"Ach ja, die Juden. Feine leute."* ("Ah yes, the Jews. Fine people.") Her father, a carpenter, had bought the place from my grandfather in the Hitlerzeit. This must have been in the early 1940s, just before he was deported to Theresienstadt and on to Auschwitz. She shared with me what she knew about where one swam in the Wesser (swimming was my mother's great love, and

I had heard a lot about the river's quick currents and what one had to do to navigate it). She told me the location of the Catholic girls' *gymnasium* that my mother had attended. I then asked her whether my wife might take a picture of me in the window in which she was sitting. (I have a picture of the house with my maternal great-grandparents in the top window, my grandparents in the middle window, and my mother and her siblings in the window where my interlocutor was sitting.) Suddenly she ceased to understand my German. The conversation was over; I could reclaim only so much.

# Recovering the Original

## Ngugi wa Thiong'o

He lay on his tummy on a high table in the assembly hall with all the students and staff present. Two teachers held his head and legs and pinned him to the table and called him monkey, as the third whip lashed his buttocks. No matter how horribly he screamed and wriggled with pain, they would not let him go. Scream Monkey. Eventually the shorts split and blood spluttered out, some of it on the shirts of those who held him down, and only then did they let him go. He stood up barely able to walk, barely able to cry, and he left, never to be seen in the precincts of that government school or any other again; I have never known what happened to him. His fault? He had been caught in the act of speaking Gĩkũyũ in the environs of the school, not once, not twice, but several times. How did the teachers come to discover his sins?

Speaking African languages in the school compound was a crime. If a student caught another speaking an African language, he would pass a token called a monitor to the culprit, who would carry it around his neck till he caught another speaking the forbidden tongues; he would pass the dreaded thing to the new culprit, and so on—children spying on one another, all day, or even tricking each other into speaking the leprous language. The one with the monitor at the end of the day was the sinner and would be punished. The above recipient of whiplashes had been a sinner for so many weeks that it looked as if he was deliberately defying the ban on Gĩkũyũ. The teachers were determined to use him as an example to teach others a lesson.

This was the Kenya of the fifties in the last century. The country was then a British settler colony, with a sizeable white settlement in the arable heartland, which they then called White Highlands. But from its colonization in 1895, Kenya was always contested, the forces of colonial occupation being met by those of national resistance, with the clash between the two sides climaxing in the armed conflict of the fifties, when Kenyans grouped around Mau Mau (or, more appropriately, Kenya Land and the Freedom Army) took to the forests and mountains to wage a guerrilla struggle against the colonial state. The outbreak of the war was preceded by a heightened nationalist cultural awareness, with songs, poetry, and newspapers in African languages abounding. The outbreak of the war was followed by a ban on performances and publications in African languages. A similar ban applied to African-run schools—they were abolished.

I first went to Kamandũra primary, a missionary set-up, in 1947. But we must have been caught up by the new nationalist awareness, because there were rumors that missionary schools were deliberately denying us children real education (*Cũth imira ciana ũgĩ*). Such schools were alleged not to be teaching Africans enough English, and some of us were pulled out of the missionary school and relocated to Manguũ, a nationalist school where the emphasis was on the history and culture of Africans. In religion, some of the nationalist schools, which called themselves independent, aligned themselves with the orthodox church, thus linking themselves to the unbroken Christian tradition of Egypt and Ethiopia, way back in the first and fourth centuries of the Christian era.

I was too young to know about this linkage; all I knew was that I was going to a school where we would be taught "deep" English alongside other subjects and languages, in our case, Gĩkũyũ. I can't remember if the English in the nationalist school was "deeper" than that taught in the previous school—I doubt if there was any difference in approach to the teaching of English—but I do recall that a composition in Gĩkũyũ was good enough to have me paraded in front of the class, in praise. That is how to write good Gĩkũyũ, the teacher said after reading it aloud to the class. So in the nationalist school of my early primary schooling, mastering Gĩkũyũ and knowing English were not in conflict. One got recognition for mastering one or both.

This peaceful co-existence of Gĩkũyũ and English in the classroom changed suddenly a few years later, when the African independent schools were shut down, with some of them resurrected as colonial state-run institutions. Manguu was one of these and the emphasis on humiliating the Gĩkũyũ language-users, as the pre-condition for acquiring English, was the most immediate outcome of the changes. It was under the new dispensation that terror was unleashed on Gĩkũyũ. The screaming student was being thrashed to take him out of the darkness of his language to the light of English knowledge.

I enjoyed English under all dispensations, but the image of the screaming student haunted me and even puzzled me for a long time. The student was hounded out of the school for speaking Gĩkũyũ, the language I had once been praised for writing well. Maybe there was something wrong with the teachers who had so praised me; the evidence of this was that they had all lost their jobs under the new colonial position on the importance of English. The new teachers, all African, all black, all Gĩkũyũ, devised all sorts of methods for associating African languages with negative images, including making linguistic sinners carry placards that asserted that they were asses. It was a war of attrition that gradually eroded pride and confidence in my language. There was nothing this language could teach me, at least nothing that could make me become educated and modern. Gore to the students who spoke Gĩkũyũ; glory to those who showed a mastery of English. I grew up distancing myself from the gore in my own language to attain the glory in English mastery.

There were rewards. A good performance in English meant success up the ladder of education. And it was this that took me from Manguũ, under its colonial tutelage, to Alliance High School, the most prestigious institution for Africans at the time, and eventually to Makerere University College in Kampala, Uganda, where I studied English Literature.

It was there, at Makerere, in the sixties—the heyday of decolonization, with country after country in Africa becoming independent—that I wrote what eventually became *The River Between*, *Weep Not Child*, and several short stories and plays, all of them in English. When later I went to Leeds University in England, I wrote the novel *A Grain of Wheat*. I truly felt joy in trying to make English words sing and capture the color and contours of my life. During the composition of *A Grain of Wheat*, much of it done in my room at Bodington, a student residence hall near the Yorkshire Moors (the setting of Brontë's *Wuthering Heights*), I often played Beethoven's Fifth Symphony in the background, and I aspired to similarly weave several movements into a seamless whole. I wanted to climb on English words to the highest peak of the mountain of human experience. But why choose English as the vehicle of my ambitions? It was not a question of choice. By this time in my education, and with everything that surrounded me at schools in Africa and abroad, writing in English seemed the most natural thing to do. I had been socialized into regarding writing in English as normal and desirable, even when the subject matter was the drama of decolonization and independence, a major theme in my work.

In all my writings I drew on the life and culture of Gīkūyū and the African peoples. Their history, particularly that of anticolonial resistance, was at the center of my writing. But this history and culture were negotiated through Gīkūyū and other African languages. Mau Mau fighters against the British colonial state, in their hideouts in the forests and mountains, did not strategize and plan in English; they talked Gīkūyū, Kiswahili, and other Kenyan languages. Yet I wrote as if they were doing so in English. I heard their voices in Gīkūyū but wrote them down in English sounds. What I was doing, of course, was a mental translation. This means that for every novel that I wrote in English, there was an original text. What happens to this original text, since in fact it exists only in the mind and is not written down? It is lost, and we can only access it through English. In my educated hands, Gīkūyū language, culture, and history came out wearing an English-language mask.

I believe there is genius in every language. It does not matter how many people speak it: the genius of a language is not dependent on the quantity of its speakers. I was taking away from the genius of Gīkūyū to add to the genius of English. I was taking away from the product of one genius to enrich the form of another.

But language is not simply an arrangement of sounds. Language is the people who speak it. There was more to my act of writing in English than simply enriching it at the expense of Gĩkũyũ. I was taking away from the people who created Gĩkũyũ and its genius, making sure that they could only access the rendering of their history through another tongue. In my early writings, I did not think about this; I was thrilled to see myself in print and reviewed in the English-language press, in Africa and abroad. But the situation was beginning to annoy me. For whom was I writing?

*A Grain of Wheat* came out in 1967. I was visiting Beirut, Lebanon, when I got a copy of the *London Observer,* which carried a tribute to the novel. The warm sentiment was the same in the rest of the press reviews. But despite the very good reception, I felt uneasy about the implications of the linguistic form. Back in Leeds, in an interview with a student newspaper, I said that after *A Grain of Wheat* I did not think I would write novels anymore. Why? Because I knew about whom I was writing but I did not know for whom I was doing it. The people about whom I wrote so eloquently would never be in a position to read the drama of their lives in their own language. On looking back, what I now find striking was that I thought of *not writing anymore* instead of switching languages to write in the one accessible to the subjects of the narratives. I still accepted English as the only possible means of my literary deliverance. What a choice is implied in my response! Write in English or not at all. And indeed my next novel, *Petals of Blood,* which came out in 1977, was written in English although littered with Gĩkũyũ and

Swahili words—almost as if, in the text, I was announcing the contradiction in my position and practice.

Two events in my life changed my relationship to English and Gĩkũyũ. In 1976, while a Professor of Literature at Nairobi University, I was invited to work at Kamĩrĩthũ Community Education and Cultural Center, a village near Limuru town, thirty or so kilometers from Nairobi. It was an education and cultural project charged with providing literacy skills and cultural material. Dramatic performance became a natural means of achieving both. The Kamĩrĩthũ community spoke Gĩkũyũ, and there was no way that we could work in the village without working in the language of the community. For the first time in my life, I was being forced by the practical needs to face the Gĩkũyũ language. *Ngaahika Ndeenda* (in English, *I Will Marry When I Want*), co-authored with Ngũgĩ wa Mirĩĩ, was the immediate outcome, and it was received warmly by the community. But it was received with hostility by the post-colonial state. The performance took place on November 11, 1977; on December 31, I was arrested by the Kenyan government and detained at Kamĩtĩ Maximum Security Prison. I have written about this in many of my books, principally *Detained: A Writer's Prison Diary*.

What I have not mentioned in those narratives is the parallel between those events at Kamĩrĩthũ in 1977 and those of my primary-school experience almost thirty years earlier. This was the first time I had been seriously engaged in writing in Gĩkũyũ since that early effort at Manguu in its nationalist phase. The teachers and the students of the nationalist school had praised me for writing in Gĩkũyũ. In the same way, the reception of the play by the community years later was fabulous. The applause in the primary school was followed by the takeover of the school by the colonial state, with terror unleashed on the speakers of the language in the school compound. The screaming student was forced out of the school. In my case, the community's applause was followed by my imprisonment; I was forced out of all class-rooms and later into exile.

It could be argued that it was my contact with Kamĩrĩĩthũ that reconnected me with the genius of Gĩkũyũ. To a certain extent, this is true. The peasantry had retained their faith in the lan-guage. They kept it alive by using it. I learnt a great deal from them. But it was in Cell 16, at a Maximum Security prison, that I really came into contact with the genius of Gĩkũyũ. I had been imprisoned by an African government for writing in an African language. Why? The question made me revisit the language, colonialism and my relationship to both. I had to find a way of connecting with the language for which I had been incarcerated. It was not a matter of nostalgia. I was not being sentimental, I needed to make that contact in order to survive. It was an act of resistance. So I wrote the very first novel ever written in Gĩkũyũ, on toilet paper, in a room provided "free" by the post-colonial state. The novel, *Caitaani Mutharabainĩ*, was published in 1980 to oral critical review. It was subsequently translated into English under the title *Devil on the Cross* and came out in 1982 to liter-ary acclaim in the English-language press—but this time only *after* it had been reviewed by the community. By the time I came out of prison in 1978, the decision had already been made. I would no longer write fiction in English (except through the translation of an existing Gĩkũyũ text); from then onwards, Gĩkũyũ would be the primary language of my creative acts. I have not looked back since.

*Devil on the Cross* was followed by *Matigari*, and I have just finished a manuscript that I started in May 1997. When *Mŭrogi wa Kagogo* comes out, it will be the longest novel ever written in Gĩkũyũ. (The English translation will be published under the title *Wizard of the Crow*.)

More important has been the rise of other novelists, poets, and playwrights in Gĩkũyũ. A new literature has been born. If this tradition has a discernible beginning and a location, it is in Cell 16, in Kenya's Kamĩtĩ Maximum Security Prison in 1977–78. Or maybe it was earlier, on the day I witnessed the plight of the screaming student. In trying to run away from his plight, perhaps I was running towards his fate. Only the genius of the language kept me alive to tell the tale.

# Split Self

## Nicholas Papandreou

Growing up bilingual meant growing up with two cultures, two opposing identities. The Greek language was, in the first case, the language of politics, meaning the speeches of my father and grandfather. "Greece to the Greeks," my father cried out in the mid-1960s; or, in my grandfather's more *apophthegmatic* (in today's parlance, sound-bite) Greek: "The King reigns but the people rule."

Greek, then, was their language, and they had a famously firm hold on it. Theirs was the language of the humble men who gathered inside our kitchen during campaigns, of modern Athenians with razor-thin ties and dark suits, of women in black with absurdly thick fingers, much thicker and stronger than my mother's or my half-Polish grandmother's. These women believed it was their god-given birthright to stretch what little of my flesh they could grab hold of.

Yet it was the language of my mother's Anglo-Saxon Chicago side that ultimately won my heart. When we moved to Greece from Berkeley in the early sixties, so my father could enter politics, English automatically became my refuge, a way to prevent the complete loss of my embryonic identity.

In *Richard the Second,* Thomas Mowbray reacts to his banishment from England: "Within my mouth you have enjailed my tongue," he says, which is "so deep a maim." Of course, my tongue was not fully imprisoned, since along with an ample supply of books, I had English as our in-house language.

I stuck solidly to my English, meaning that I read British books (and learned to say *Bloody 'ell* and *Blimey!*—which I was sure derived from a British rendition of *Blame me!*) but also introduced comic-book expressions when beating up my younger brother, Andy. My less-than-Homeric blows to his small chest were accompanied by rapturous cries of "zap!" "pow!" and, for the execution, "kablooey!" I was always delighted to discover new words, especially slang. When an American teenager asked me where the toilet was so he could "take a leak," I was bowled over. I imagined our bodies to be like badly built ships from which water leaked out. When an American family moved in next door—I learned later the father helped put mine in jail—I learned that "man" could be thrown into a sentence just about anywhere, and that "cool" meant, well, cool, man.

Yet Greek was all around, with classes in geometry, algebra, and geography, in a version of the language known as "katharevousa" (meaning clean or pure). The language brought with it all the attendant cultural sidebars: priests grilled alive by Turks, women who jumped off cliffs rather than be taken by the enemy, and the Bridge of Arta, which reminded me of the story of Sisyphus—the bridge would be fixed in the day but would collapse at night, and so a virgin was built into the bridge and this successfully reversed the trend. There was also the story of the World War Two collaborator who chopped off and then sold partisans' heads to the Germans like cabbage. When the war was over the man was caught, sliced lightly all over his skin with razor blades, then buried in a sand dune in Thessaly.

I couldn't wait to tell my friends "back home" about the lamb we had for a pet, about the sheer steepness of the Isthmus of Corinth, about the shark I saw hanging by a hook on the island of Hydra, about the taste of souvlaki with pita and the caterpillars that hung in white sacks from the branches of pine trees. There were soon no friends on the other side, yet I was still possessed by the need to tell them everything that was different from America. It took me years to realize that I carried the other side with me at all times.

But I was most impressed by the enormous crowds that came to listen to my father and my grandfather, through whom I learned and imitated a rhetorical speech-making Greek. "Greece of Christian Greeks catholically protestant," my grandfather hurled at the dictators when he was under house arrest. Even then, at the age of eleven, I marveled at how he squeezed three religions into one active phrase. Other sayings of his joined the pantheon of national tradition: *Many a people has deposed a king, never has a king deposed the people,* or *All regimes boast political parties, only democracies have opposition parties.* The rhetorical expertise of both men put pressure on me to speak a Greek that was better than the average—a pressure so daunting that, I now realize, I soon abandoned the effort and threw myself squarely into the camp of the possible.

I remember selecting from my parents' library the thickest book I could find, presumably because the thickest book would provide me the greatest protection, which is how I ended up reading, at the age of nine, the sorry life of an architect written by someone with an unpronounceable first name (Ayn Rand's

*Fountainhead*). But I quickly strayed into the adventures of Biggles and Blyton's Secret Five, the Hardy Boys and every single Drew Sisters book I could secure from my sister, Gayle-Sophia. I refused to call her Sophia and persisted in her nicely American Gayle (after the actress Gail Storm, whom my parents had apparently taken a liking to in the fifties, when she was born). The rest of us had solidly Greek names: Nick, Andy, George.

It was my godfather, also a George, who got me thinking more about language. "Why is a spoon called a spoon?" he asked.

"That's silly," I recall answering. "Because it's a spoon! And that's a fork, so it's called a fork!"

I hadn't yet realized that he was a fan of Magritte's. I liked my godfather because he looked precisely the way a godfather should look: three-piece suits, a smart tie, a hat, a cane, a well-trimmed mustache, with a distinct air of aristocracy.

"Do you know what your name means?" he asked me when we sat in the dining room in our home in Paleo Psycheko.

"My name means . . . well, it means Nick!"

"But in its full version," he offered, "what does it really mean?"

"You mean Nicholas?"

"Two words in there. Can you see them?"

"No."

"Nike and Laos, victor of the people."

"Cow!" (I didn't know the whole expression yet.) So Greek words really did have secrets.

I was off. I easily pried apart brother George's first name: *geo* for earth and *orge* for the verb plough—though I had to look *orge* up. George was no more nor less than a farmer. Little Andy with his blond hair and the black tuft sprouting out from the crown, who actually spoke only Greek, had a name that meant simply Man, like Oriana Fallaci's book *Un Uomo,* about her Greek lover. Sophia, however, didn't have a synthetic name and hers meant simply Wisdom. Names like hers were less fun because there was no puzzle, no secret.

The baker's wife, Euphony, was fair game. When my sister once came home with a loaf of bread, I shouted: "You phony! I bet you didn't buy it from Mrs. Good-Sound!" Alexander, a friend, meant Man-Repellent. Thinking I was ahead of the game, I challenged my mother (who was having a harder time with Greek than I was) by demanding she tell me a word I didn't know, in any language. She threw out an easy one at first— "sludge," I think it was—which I proceeded to answer. Then came a far more difficult one, which I still remember to this day, amazed she knew such a long word. It was the word "eleemosynary." I admitted defeat. "Look it up," she advised. I discovered, to my delight, it had a Greek root—*eleimosini,* meaning the quality of being charitable or charitableness.

I began to look for English words which were in fact Greek— except that you would never think they were. I made a list of such words: For example, the word "cemetery" *(kimitirio)* simply meant a sleeping place. The word "police," familiar the world over, derived from the word *polis.* The word "zone" was the Greek word for what we wore around our waist—a belt. My all-time favorite is a word you'd never think was Greek: "disaster," meaning a bad alignment of the stars.

I started to drive the family nuts by finding words that either sounded awful or made a lot of noise when you said them loudly, since I had now become the most word-infected family member:

"Dad, stop making all that *cacophony*!"

"Mom, that souvlaki's really gonna hurt my *esophagus*!"

"I can't concentrate with all the *susurrus* from your newspaper!"

"Dad, sometimes you are a *pompous* pop!"

For a brash statement like that I could get popped myself, since my father, especially on his return from America, was growing less and less beholden to American child psychologists and had reverted more and more to the traditional forms of control—Ottoman law, as we called it, applied sporadically but effectively with the help of a *zoni* (belt) to our behinds.

Once I had worked out first names (*Cleanthes*—Bouquet, *Calliope*—Beautiful-faced), there appeared a whole new treasure where I least expected it: Greek surnames. My sister and I would translate surnames to see how dumb they sounded in English: Mister Kalovelonis was Mister Goodneedle, while Mister Kalambokis was his Royal Highness Mister Corn. Our all-time favorites were the derogatory surnames like Mrs. Low-Butt and Mrs. Fat-butt, the famous Buttley sisters, like my mother's high-school heroines, the Andrews Sisters.

The last name of one of my father's deputies made no sense but was certainly fun to say, if you could spit it out without stuttering: *Papapanayotou*. Three pa's in a row—try them apples on for size. Our surname, with its double papa (our great-grandfather was a priest, hence the Papa) was nothing compared to Mister Papapanayotou. My gleeful rendition of his name each day caused his name to be repeated by nearly all the household. "Oh dear Mister Papapanayotou," my mother might exclaim for no reason.

When he showed up one night, my father made a big thing of introducing him to me, then did me the awesome favor of actually adding yet another "pah" to the train. For days I savored the delightful extra—Papa-pa!-panayotou. I don't think the owner of the surname thought twice about this delicious distortion, but I treasured it for weeks and kept seeing my father's slight grin as he machine-gunned the whole thing into the hallway, specifically for my pleasure. In a way I was being acknowledged as the family's linguist.

During the dictatorship of 1967–1974, with my father in jail, we called on the American side of the family to visit us. One such member was a medal-studded Lieutenant Colonel who had just returned from service in Vietnam. Walking around Athens with all six-foot-five of him, in full military decoration, ignoring curfew, we were able finally to stand outside Averoff prison on Alexandras Street, where my father was being held. This was not just a thrill, a small act of revenge; it also reinforced the sense that English offered much more protection than did Greek.

We moved to Sweden in 1968, after my father, with the help of President Johnson—who was quoted as saying, in full Texan drawl, "Let that damn sunuvabitch out"—was amnestied by the dictators. A twelve-year-old loosed on Stockholm, I dipped briefly but excitedly into the Englishness of Swedish. Besides the blatant and unheard of pix of full-breasted vix which hung on just about every newsstand in the city, I was transfixed by the word for entrance and exit—the blatancy of the *infart* and *utfart* strewn all over the place. Adolescence is nothing if not delight in the scatological (Greek for "study of excrement," as opposed to eschatological, "the theology of death or endings"). My favorite: the word for constipation in Swedish was *ferstoppning*, meaning exactly what it says, thank you.

On the run, we finally ended up in Canada in the last year of the decade, under the good graces of the then Prime Minister Pierre Trudeau, who offered political asylum to my father if he wouldn't overdo his criticism of America (a restraint my father was unable to obey). Strangely enough—or perhaps not so strangely—my real home, the one I thought of as my real home was for many years the country of Canada. And Canadians— well, they spoke pretty much like we did but, to my great delight, not exactly. When I played basketball, the referee might shout "Eeyoot of Bounds!" Objects were "yea high," highways had "soft shoulders," and a decent-sized snowplow weighed "two ton" without the pluralizing ess. You could talk like you were a hardware employee showing a customer the goods and get away with it: "Well, there you've got *your* Phillips Screw and *your* five-inch dead bolt . . ." The wonderful possessive *your* gave you instant ownership over all such male objects. There was also a machine called a "snowblower" which, besides snow, would churn out pebbles, animals and, in at least one James Bond film, a couple of bad humans. Ski-Doos raced across the snow at night in the vast white space: an upgraded version of Dr. Zhivago.

Going to school in rural Ontario—where, for some reason that I never discovered, my father decided we should live—I learned that the business end of a scythe was called a *snath*, that Viceroy butterflies look like Monarchs but don't have the same flight pattern, and that Lord Strathcona drove the last spike of the Canadian Pacific Railway on November 7, 1885. Swamps were called *muskegs,* a frozen pond thundered when you walked on it, trapped air bubbles looked like crystal balls, a hockey puck traveled up to a hundred miles an hour, a solid slapshot was as satisfying as any slam dunk, and, contrary to popular wisdom, when it got really cold it didn't snow. Driving along Route 13 in King City one cold afternoon, we passed the small *kimitirio* with its snow-laden crosses sticking up like frozen spinning jacks. I turned to my mother. "Mom, when I die, this is where I want to be buried." Not in Berkeley, not in Greece, not in Sweden, but here, in King City, Ontario. I had never seen her cry before because of something I said.

It was in Canada I first heard a third but instantly recognizable language, one which I sort of knew without ever having learned it. It was the English spoken by first-generation Greeks, what the community of bi-culturals like me now informally calls Cringlish. Gringlish usually takes English verbs or even nouns and pops them directly into the sentence. Will you park the car becomes, in Gringlish, "Tha kanis *park* to *caro*?" How many blocks away do you live becomes "Posa blockya makria?"

I dislike the word *Gringlish* because it sounds like a combination of two evil heroes, Grendel and the Grinch. I prefer a word of my own invention, which is perhaps derogatory but more to the point: Dinerese. In the Greek diners spread across Route One, in Chicago or in Florida, in perhaps the most famous Greek eatery of all, Astoria's Neptune Diner (nested neatly beneath the Triborough Bridge), you can still hear this language. "The Greek people," a phrase much liked and much used by my father, in Dinerese becomes "the Greek peep." Greeks love the peep. Peeps of the world unite. Long live the peep. Fast-speaking Greeks dismiss the distance between words. Like a hut kupukuffee? No, you sumunabeets?

My favorite interchange occurred while I was in college, when a Greek Greek who had learned English only from his law books and who worked part-time at a Greek pizza place in New Haven encountered an unhyphenated America. The conversation went something like this, as best as I can recall:

"Ordered a double cheese 'zah, half-pep, half anch."

"I am sorry. What was that?"

"Half-pep half-anch, man. The full spread."

"I'm sorry. I don't speak colloquial."

"You don't speak what?"

"Slang. That's it. I don't speak slang."

"Who's speaking slang? I'm speaking English."

"Do you mock me, sir? Do you deride me?"

"C'mon, man! I just want my 'zah!"

"You think you're in your home, that you can talk like this?"

"Man, this ain't no home, this is Naples effing Pizza last time I looked. Which planet you from?"

"Planet is the ancient Greek word for wanderer, sir. I know precisely my origins, sir, from Arta, in Western Greece, sir, where they once built the bridge."

"Sheesh! Get back on that ship and return to wherever!"

Strangely enough, the Greek I had learned as a kid in the "home" country was a passport into restaurants, brought instant connections in college with others whose surnames began with *Papa* or ended with *opoulos,* and afforded me instant, no-questions-asked entry into a distinctly raunchy world of nightclubs owned or run by Greeks: Mykonos, Zorba's or, in Baltimore, Towson Bouzouki.

The burden of the Greek language weighed heavily on me because, more and more, I was being called on to represent my father, who in the late seventies now led the chief opposition party, bent on bringing socialism to Greece. I attended "caucuses" on Cyprus, helped organize the Greeks At Yale (lovely acronym for that), and gave numerous fund-raising speeches in hardcore Greek-American communities located in Astoria, Baltimore or Chicago. I was a stand-in for my father, who was climbing the steps to the palace of power. One place to which I was obliged to return time and again was the Crystal Palace in Astoria, Queens. Here I could find the whole enchilada of Greek-American linguistic abortions. The Crystal Palace was the prime location for thousands of Greek-American events over two to three decades: political rallies, wedding receptions, dances, baptisms—a Coppolian ethnic-American setting of sheer kitsch. Much later I realized that there once existed a real Crystal Palace, built over a hundred and fifty years ago in England, "the crystal edifice that can never be destroyed," as Dostoyevsky puts it in *The Underground Man*. Though I am no longer enmeshed in that particular strain of ethnic America called Astoria, and though Astoria has now lost much of its Greekness, I drew some meaning from this indirect link to the Russian writer, even if the meaning is no greater than a micro nano bit.

By the age of twenty-nine, I had acquired yet another language. A Ph.D. in economics taught me everything there was to know about *transcendental logarithmic cost functions, variance covariance matrices* and *three stage least squares estimators*. Never having returned to Greece except for summers until my studies were completed, I returned for my military service in the late eighties, exactly a week after defending my doctorate on a comfortable Ivy League campus.

That's how I found myself on the island of Lemnos, in Northern Greece, inducted into the Greek Air Force. I could have relied on my American citizenship to avoid military service altogether, but such an act would have been highly unpatriotic; besides, I actually liked the idea of wearing a uniform and carrying a gun and not reading another economics article. There was also this: I imagined bumping into an officer who had arrested my father the night of the coup, the same one who had pointed a machine gun at my face. The thought excited me. I am sorry to report that such a meeting never occurred and that the extreme right-wing officers saluted me as I did them.

The island was honed of volcanic rock, the home of Poseidon. The barracks were full of raw eighteen-year-olds most of whom spoke with distinct regional accents. I immediately felt like an intruder, a jokester, a false twin who would soon be discovered for pretending to be the Prime Minister's son. I lived, thought and wrote in English, yet my father was by now not only Prime Minister but also Minister of Defense. This made him head honcho of all soldiers. As the son of the nationalist leader, I was supposed to be the automatic expert on all matters Greek, to know the Heroes of the Revolution, to know which minister served what post and what year, and, worst of all, to make no spelling mistakes on all documents for which I was responsible.

Yet for all the pressure, there was one tremendous benefit for a word-infected person like me: army slang. Greek army slang.

"With someone else's ass it's easy to pretend you're gay," I heard one soldier say after returning from a particularly cold night shift. Another soldier who'd stubbed his toe at night on the bunkbeds shouted: "Screw the donkey that ate Christ's palm fronds on the road to Nazareth!" If you dropped your rifle you would most likely think of God and shout, "Screw the Virgin Mary's ear!" (This was a reference to Immaculate Conception; certain Fathers of the Church once held that such a conception had occurred via the good Mary's auricular orifice.)

Not that the soldiers had no sense of their ancient heritage:

"Halt! Who goes!"

"Friend!"

"What did Ulysses say when he got to Ithaca?"

"Screw me!"

Or:

"How did Ulysses spy on the Trojans?"

"Through the wooden horse's wooden butthole."

We also used more standard passwords: Hercules-Lion, Achilles-Patroclus, Sophocles-Oedipus—things the Turks, the enemy about fifty kilometers away, were supposed to have no idea about and could never answer properly, even if they had wanted to.

My greatest fear at the time was to be called up in front of the thousand or so soldiers to say the Lord's Prayer. Because of all the back and forth between countries, I had missed the teaching of it in either language and for the life of me couldn't remember it. Each night, as we were all standing in line, the commander would call out a name at random and ask the specified "grunt" to come recite the prayer. While waiting for the name to be called, I would try to remember the prayer, filling in the empty Greek parts with what I remembered in English, then translating it back into Greek. But this was a puzzle best not done under pressure, next to a thousand breathing bodies. Fortunately, the stars were not once in disorder. My name was never called.

All this was a rich linguistic pillow in which to sleep at night. When I finally decided to write, I saw that the friction of the two languages had great value and could convert the trivial into the metaphorically rich. A clever person is an "eagle's talon," a tall man is a "Cypress-lad," a piano is a "tooth-mattress," the earth is an "ant-sphere," a boy's erect penis is a "fakir's flute." "Never scowl at the lowest steps," a saying goes, "since you need them to get to the palace."

I discovered rhyming couplets from the island of Crete which I tried to translate:

*Others shrivel up from the times, the wars and years*
*but me, I shrivel up with the pains and the fears.*

*The wind beats my clothes and the sun eats my knives*
*and a small little love eats up my insides.*

There was gold then in them thar hills. "I can hear the salty smell," a village woman once told me when the wind brought with it bits of the sea. I was shocked by the confounding of the senses, and later learned that she had just expressed what philosophers call "synesthesia," where one sense "leaks into" the other. (Ah, there's that unexpected four-letter word coming back at me.) A more literary example of a synesthete is Nabokov, who in his autobiography *Speak, Memory,* tells of seeing colors when he hears the alphabet pronounced—a trait he refers to as "colored hearing," or *audition coloré* in French, which, I guess, sounds more sophisticated.

My Greek grandmother, Sophia Mineiko Papandreou, half-Greek and half-Polish, offered me a name of someone she once knew, a little girl named Eulalia. She told me it came from the prefix *ef*, meaning good, and *lalia*, meaning speech. It was a name I found much later in my readings of Americans from the South, when I decided to become a writer myself. I did actually meet a Eulalia, on the island of Syros, with its Catholic and Orthodox churches jutting up into the sky competing for space. I was presenting my first book, *A Crowded Heart,* written in English but available in Greek translation. The crowd was decent-sized. After all, my surname guaranteed me instant recognition, and one effect was a small but constant crowd at my book readings.

An aging actor, Constantine, had been chosen to read a section from my book. He read it as if it were ancient Greek tragedy, shouting at the top of his voice, and once the applause subsided—an applause which was obliged to rival his efforts—he sat down next to me. While others continued to speak about my book (the mayor, a deputy from my father's party, a high-school teacher with two books of poetry under his belt, and god knows how many others), he struck up a conversation with me as if we weren't on the podium. I kept hunching lower in the hope this would induce him to lower his voice. Suddenly he squeezed my thigh excitedly. "See that girl there, over there, with the dark hair and those eyes? You see her? She once had a speech impediment but I corrected it with four years of lessons in orthophony. Take one guess what her name is." That's how I met the only Eulalia I have ever known. I even got the chance to sign her name in my book, which I did with a calligraphic flourish. She was indeed a tall, dark-haired beauty and she did indeed speak with perfect diction, the way a Eulalia should, but nope, I never saw her again.

*Lalia* in Greek means voice or language or tongue. In the Swedish the word for Speak is *tala*. *Tala svensk?* In Danish *lalle* is a drunken person's babble. When I started to learn some Spanish I thought I heard an echo of *lalia* in *habla*, with that *la* at the end of it. From a Brazilian acquaintance I heard *fala* for talk. Think *parler*. Or even parlance.

One summer, back in Greece between college years, I visited the pine-filled island of Skiathos. A fisherman took me to his favorite beach, Lalaria. "Why is it called Lalaria?" I asked.

He had an answer (when doesn't a Greek?). "You see those rocks there?" He pointed to the large round stones like ostrich eggs that formed the beach. "When the sea hits those stones they talk. La la. Close your eyes and listen."

I think all members of my family are wounded by language in one way or another. Brother George, in the words of his detractors, "is our first Minister of Foreign Affairs who actually speaks a *second* language—Greek." My mother doesn't do television interviews because she is worried she will place a feminine pronoun to a masculine noun, and this after leading the Greek women's movement for decades. My sister has escaped to Canada and her little son now speaks fluent Canadian. For a long time, my younger brother Andreas prepared his economics classes at the university down to the last word, so that he wouldn't make any grammatical mistakes. My father, always burdened with the suspicion that he was too American, commanded both languages fluently. Ironically enough, he was perhaps the only member who never suffered from the mistake bird of language.

I now treasure the split. English acts as a passport into unexplored territory, into the terrain of my fictional Greece, into the Greece of my memory, the Greece of my childhood.

# Limpid, Blue, Poppy

## M. J. Fitzgerald

In early 1959, while we were living in a small seaside town along the Ligurian coast, Italian television made a documentary of us. The documentary was called *Una famiglia Americana in Italia*— An American family in Italy.

The decision by the fledgling RAI to make such a documentary may have had a lot to do with the reversal: an American family in Italy rather than the thousands of Italian families forced to emigrate to America. But I imagine that one of the reasons they chose our family from what was not an insignificant population of Americans in Italy was that we were not in fact living an expatriate life in Milan, Florence, or Rome, among larger or smaller clusters of other Americans, but were living integrated in the small-town life of Levanto, the only Americans there year round.

A second irresistible reason in that children-loving country must surely have been the presence of a clutch of six duckling children, three boys and three girls, all more or less the same age (there is a mere seven years between the oldest of us and the youngest), all pale and freckly, all fair-haired and, like all children, all absolutely deserving of the bruising pinch on the cheek and the exclamation "bella!" Of the four of us who were in school, three went to the local elementary school: the two boys in the boys' section, I across the green-and-white-tiled corridor in the girls' section. My older sister was at boarding school at Trinità de' Monti in Rome, an exclusive enough place run by French nuns, where the student population consisted of fewer than a hundred daughters of the higher middle classes, mostly from the poorer south—Calabria, Puglia, Basilicata, Campania, Sicilia—but with a sprinkling from the more northern regions and from Lazio itself. By the time I joined her briefly in 1963, there were a couple of Americans with whom I walked in irrepressible sobs to the American Consulate to sign the condolence book following the 22nd of November. But there were none when she went in the fall of 1958.

A third consideration may have been my father's status as *Il Professore* who seemed not to have a job—he made a poem of my brother's famous boast among his peers that the reason why *il babbo* was at home all day was that at night he was a burglar—even though the study where he spent his days translating the allocated lines of Homer's *Odyssey* was an inviolate place we were rarely privileged to visit. The running of the household was squarely on my mother's shoulders, with the help of two live-in maids, Maria and Alice. Each went home once a month to villages high in the Ligurian mountains, with ten dollars for their families.

For months, it seemed, a television crew came and went, stayed days or perhaps it was weeks, then left and then returned. I remember having to walk again and again down the brick and stone stairway that led up to the olive and vine grove behind the house. I remember being incapable of sitting still in class with hands behind my back, before they were to film me playing *Für Elise* on the piano with my father. I remember dashing in and out of my father's study: it took what seemed like hours to set up the piano just for the filming.

I stopped taking piano lessons shortly after, many months before we gathered in the priest's house to see the documentary. As my father predicted when he sighed at my stubbornness—I don't want to, I hate it, I don't care—I regret it today with as much intensity as I then detested the dull *solfeggi*, the thump of the right hand on the left to achieve a metronome beat, and the endless repetition of the scales. I am pretty sure now that I pouted and stomped and insisted in Italian, and that my father expressed his regret and disappointment in English. But I have no memory of it. The only memory I have of this use of two languages is that when my parents did not want us to understand something, they would spell it out in English. We understood their speech in English completely, but spelling, reading, and writing defeated us all until we were in our teens and had begun the migration to the English-speaking world.

In the early fall of 1959, before school started in October, we moved to Florence, and for three years we rented the *piano nobile* of the Brewster villa: the priest's house was attached to the small chapel that was itself a wing of the villa. Sometime in late 1959 or 1960—I have a dim memory of rain and chill, so it may have been the winter—we crowded into the parlor with a number of other folk who did not have television sets, and sat on the sagging sofa or the hard straw chairs or the jute-covered brick floor to watch the documentary. My parents took small sips of the artichoke cordial Cynar, the *digestivo* that was the preferred after-dinner drink to offer guests in modest households, and we were offered *caramelle* under the disapproving eye of our mother, helpless to fight the rules of hospitality which required candy to be distributed to children on great occasions.

Only the setting has stayed with me from that very first viewing—that, and the inch-long hard fruit candy with the soft center, wrapped in crinkly cellophane. It was suddenly in every *Bar* and *Alimentari,* but I had never tasted it before, and it immediately replaced my favorite *mentine*—the tiny sugar drops in various flavors that are miraculously still for sale in Levanto. The word *candy* does nothing to my taste buds, whereas the word *caramella* brings instantly back the sweet crunch of the teeth through the shell, softened by sucking for as long as possible, to the soft center.

I did not see the documentary again for over twenty-five years, not until my father was diagnosed with cancer and undertook the six-month-long battle to contain the spread from the lungs to the liver. I spent long days with him in the summer of 1984, while he fought the losing campaign with chemotherapy and radiation. My brother succeeded in spiriting a copy of the sixteen-millimeter documentary from the archives of RAI, had it formatted to tape, and had copies made. He came by with the copy for my father on a beautiful summer afternoon: the sun shone on the canvas shades without dazzling its way in, merely giving a fullness of white light to the quiet sick room. My brother and I flanked our father as he lay on the hospital bed that could be raised and lowered. He sat up a little, his legs over the folded end of the mattress, his back and head against the raised top of the mattress, and we watched the official, thirty-minute-long edition of our life twenty-five years before.

The most startling thing at that second viewing was how very halting my parents' Italian was. But whereas my mother valiantly improvised her way through the hesitation and the mistakes into comprehensibility, my father was utterly dependent on the note pad he kept glancing at as he spoke to the interviewer, and his pronunciation was atrocious. As I sat by him in the muted summer light, I realized with shock that as an adult, after I had learnt English, after our family migrated back to the United States and then broke up, I had not heard him speak Italian, and save for the occasional, absolutely untranslatable word, I had not spoken to him in Italian. With my mother it was a constant slide between the two languages, used easily and interchangeably. Her Italian was strongly accented, but she would speak it whenever she could. My father seemed to me at that moment to have abandoned Italian as completely as he had our family life.

I glanced at him beside me on the sickbed he would not rise from, his beautiful nose ever more aquiline in the gaunt features, the green of his eyes darker in the deepening sockets, the long expressive thumb at rest from its characteristic gesture—forming a circle with the middle finger while he clicked his tongue against the roof of his mouth to make a point. After all, it was twenty years since the migration started in the fall of 1964, when he took up his position at Harvard; twenty years since the four eldest of his children had been dispersed to boarding schools in four different countries. Childhood in Italy, the momentous source of experience and impression that had determined so much of my life, the eleven years between October 1953 and October 1964, were no more than a brief interlude in the life of my parents, an interlude that my mother clung to, and that my father had shaken off. Perhaps he never did speak Italian with us? Perhaps he spoke in English, and it was sufficient for him to understand the Italian we spoke to communicate with us?

The tape came to an end and my father grinned at us, sighed deeply, but made no comment. Embarrassed at his lack of fluency in the language I spoke as fluently as English, I did not think then to ask him whether he had ever spoken to us in Italian at all. Although he watched the documentary a number of times with the rotation of siblings who were in and out as constantly as I was during those last months, he and I never watched it again together, neither during the rest of that last summer when I was there for days at a time, nor in the blaze of the red and yellow fall, when I would fly back from England regularly to be with him. I have seen it only once since then. I will perhaps look at it again before I finish the composition of this piece. I feel a strong reluctance to do so, partly from a measure of shame at our privileged life—a shame engendered by a political correctness I simultaneously view with great suspicion. And partly I am reluctant for reasons I cannot quite articulate, as nebulous as my fear of the ache of nostalgia and as clear as the possibility of the stab of regret at the loss and then the death of my father. And now there is the rawer bereavement at the recent death of my mother: in my memory of the documentary, she still wears the long Native American braids she had in the photos of us taken on the beach in Sestri Levante and Levanto.

When an assortment of us coincided by my father's bedside, we talked about the documentary and remembered those years, which were by then really the only link between all of us. But the talking, I see now, came from us, not from him. As I write, I realize that he had supplied a context for our whole lives that was not only not his, but that was as distant from his background as it could possibly be. The blue of the Mediterranean, the dazzling light of heat refracting, the arid steep slopes of the olive groves, the ground that brought to the surface more stone with each rainfall—gathered daily *per fare una casa,* to make a home, by the sweetly retarded son of the *contadino* who looked after those trees and picked the olives and the grapes— the acrid smell of the *mosto* in the barn where we too trod and gleefully squashed the grapes with bare and dancing feet, the delicate scent of mimosa, the medlar we climbed into, the hydrangea whose leaves made crowns, and the ubiquitous pines and magnolias—what had they in common with the landlocked Midwest of the United States, of which I knew nothing in 1984 except that corn grew as high as an elephant's eye? What did our childhood days filled with sibling squabbles and friendships have in common with the small household in which my father grew up against the backcloth of a loss too huge to fathom, the death of his mother and brother?

It is such a different context from mine that it has only been possible for me even to begin to comprehend it since my own motherhood has shown me how the loss of me would affect my son, and since life's turn has dragged me kicking and screaming to the same landlocked Midwest, mere hours away from my father's birthplace, Springfield, Illinois, where he lived those all-important years to adolescence in the singular quiet companionship of an ailing father, with winters of ice-skating in a dazzle of deep snow rather than summers of snorkeling through a dazzle of sea. A sea whose intensity of blue can only be contained in the Italian word *azzurro.* The word *blue,* an anodyne descriptive term, does not convey that childhood sea, but *azzurro* brings it all back with a violence in memory that invariably hits me like a punch in the stomach.

I think now, as I write and look back at us watching *Una famiglia Americana in Italia* on that sunny afternoon of his last summer, that perhaps my father never left the Midwest—unlike my mother, who truly did leave Texas and actively chose the life she led. I think that perhaps my father merely found himself migrating from Springfield to Choate, to Harvard, to New York, to New England, to Italy; just as I feel I have never truly left Italy and have simply found myself migrating from country to country, borne by necessity rather than driven by choice.

But what about the choice I made *not* to read or speak Italian? It was a very deliberate decision, taken in the wake of the earnest aspiration to "be a writer." I had to choose between the two languages, but why did I not choose Italian? At sixteen, when the decision was taken, Italian and English were in equipoise—if anything, Italian was the language in which I was more fluent. After two years at boarding school in England, my spoken English still suffered from Italian intonations, and my written English from errors consequent on an Italianate and Latinate sentence construction.

I had always been a ravenous reader, although never a precocious one: at seven I lived on a regular diet of *Piccole Donne, Piccole Donne Crescono, I ragazzi di Jo* (Little Women) and *Heidi.* At eight I read *Cuore* perhaps a hundred times. At ten I read in Italian the pre-teen bright blue hardbacks about English boarding schools that I could buy for five hundred lire (stolen, I'm afraid, from my mother's handbag) at the newspaper kiosk at the bottom of the tree-lined avenue that led to the square where we lived in Florence. And after we moved to Perugia in the fall of 1961, I read every single one of the hundred or so books the previous owner of our house left behind: 1930s paperback editions of Emilio Salgari as well as romances by forgotten authors, in one of which a turbaned and bearded man converted to Mahomet to be able to reach the woman he loved in a harem . . . I did not at twelve read *I Promessi Sposi,* or *Mastro Don Gesualdo,* or the whole *Iliad,* or even the whole of the *Zabaglione,* extracts of all of which we were reading in our first year of secondary school. I did not read Pavese, Sciascia, Bassani, Buzzati, or even Calvino, whose *Fiabe Italiane* would provide the final impetus fifteen years later for "Creases," the first story I wrote that defined my ambition as a writer. The determining book at thirteen, during my eighteen months at boarding school in Rome, was a three-volume novel translated into Italian from German, of a decidedly satisfying symmetry: A gifted Austrian violinist of seventeen marries a man exactly twice her age. They have twin girls who are seventeen in the second volume, where they meet and marry twins. In the third volume their children in turn are seventeen, and the saga ends with the girl of the first volume, now an old woman of roughly my present age, playing the violin after her husband's death at sixty-eight, overheard by her thirty-four-year-old children and seventeen-year-old grandchildren.

During that year, 1963, I wrote my first novel. In Italian, of course. A gifted teenage pianist dying of leukemia meets a girl whose boarding school abuts his hospice, and a doomed romance blossoms between them . . . or maybe *she* is dying of leukemia and is consoled by his wonderful playing of Chopin from the conservatory which abuts the hospice. It was a short novel, the hard-won length of a notebook, written in collaboration with two schoolmates during the endless evening homework hours, and laboriously typed out on my father's Olivetti 22 during school holidays. I wrote poems then, too, in Italian: all critiqued by my classmates with comments ranging from *mi piace* to *bella* to *carina.*

But I remember also the misery of those days. The school did not have a library, and the random selection of books on random shelves scattered here and there around the school was so quickly devoured that I had nothing new to read. And whereas in my childhood I had been content to read the same book over and over again, by then I wanted a new book every day. Even when I got home for the holidays, the situation was no better. There were shelves and shelves of unreadable English books, but the supply of Italian ones had run out, and there was no kiosk at the end of the avenue where I could replenish my supply with stolen money: in Perugia, the only stores within walking distance in the poor village above the house were a meager *Alimentari* always swarming with flies, and a general goods store that only stocked the photo-romances I was explicitly forbidden to get. I remember trying in vain to slow my reading down so that I would not come to the end of a beloved book (*Le cinque Sorelle d'America,* for example, Five American Sisters) and have to scour to find something I had not read.

*Al centro,* where we would saunter sometimes up and down the length of the cobbled main street in the early evening, from the Duomo to Piazza Italia and back to the Duomo—the *passeggiata* I was just beginning to dimly know as an occasion for flirting and courtship—there were two bookstores. But even there, no book appealed to me; they were either the same blue-backed hardbacks I had bought with stolen money in Florence, or uninspiring grown-up novels. New *Gialli Mondadori*, the detective and murder mysteries that had superseded stories of stowaway children in English country houses as reading that could be bought from newspaper kiosks, only appeared once a month or so. I would have devoured one of those in the car on the twenty-minute ride home, if the road had not been so winding it would have made me car-sick. I certainly devoured them before falling asleep, incapable of putting them down until the mystery had been solved. And then time stretched out in an eternity of not reading. The crossword puzzles in *La Settimana Enigmistica* and the random accumulation of odd facts that made up much of the rest of the weekly publication, with its impossible rebus and the silly cartoons, did not substitute for the deep immersion in lives not my own that took place when I was reading a novel. Nor did reading *Grazia* or *La Domenica del Corriere* whenever I could lay my hands on them, nor did the comic books, although *Topolino, Nembo Kid,* and *Tex Willer* were always around— demanded by my siblings as earnestly as I demanded the *Gialli* from the newspaper kiosk—and I did read them. I had even been driven to reading the Jack London novels that my friend Luciana thrust on me, and which I did not enjoy at all: adventure was not my dream as much as romance.

Just at this moment of cusp, in my second teenage year, as the world of childhood receded so rapidly I did not even have occasion to regret it, I was sent to the longed-for boarding school in England. We did not have the grey uniforms with coveted striped ties, but we did have to wear berets and blazers. Eventually I even indulged in midnight feasts of crumpets and marmite washed down with the cider I did not like but pretended to, and the beer I could not even pretend to like. Eventually I did get into trouble for smoking in my room. But the great revelation of English boarding school was not social—I was too fundamentally introverted for that. It was literary. We read *A Midsummer Night's Dream* and especially *Romeo and Juliet,* which satisfied every particle of my dreamy, romantic, and sentimental heart. We read *Jane Eyre.* There had been nothing like *Jane Eyre* in my reading so far. None of the romantic heroes of the 1930s novels in the attic of our house, or the stories in the hybrid magazines of photo-romances that I hid under the mattress whenever I had managed to sneak one home, had ever been blinded or handicapped in any way: the passion that I had felt at twelve for Leopardi, because he was a great *hunchback* poet, was finally being justified. And then I read *Wuthering Heights.* Bad brooding Heathcliff, how I loved you: as much as Catherine did, both of us with all of our misguided romantic hearts and souls.

Boarding school was the perfect setting for me. As long as I did as I was told when I was told to do it, I was left alone. I basked in that friendly indifference. The library had shelf after shelf of books that appealed to me—Georgette Heyer, Agatha Christie, Charlotte Brontë, Kathleen Winsor, Emily Brontë. To access them, all I had to do was learn to read English as quickly as I was learning, after the first mute months, to speak it. Patricia Highsmith, Dorothy Sayers; by the end of my second year, *Pride and Prejudice* and the wonderful revelation of Jane Austen's astringent romanticism; George Eliot's ocean-sized scope in *Middlemarch;* Shakespeare's *Antony and Cleopatra; Twelfth Night,* with Viola and her doppelgänger brother both in love, and an end as satisfying as the ending of the three-volume saga of my twelfth year, but in a language that exactly mirrored the excessive drama in my heart.

Returning to Italian writing after gorging on this diet of English—Leopardi's *L'Infinito* was restrained in comparison to Dylan Thomas's *Fern Hill*—was like returning to milk toast after scones with clotted cream. I loved the accumulation of adjectives that a language so rich in words could indulge in, instead of the nuances in the repetition of the same adjective that gives Italian its power. I loved the exaggeration of English, the curlicues of language, its baroque quality. Many of the churches, much of the painting, and people's gesturing in Italy are baroque. But the language itself is severe: its beauty lies in elegant simplicity and the hypnotic power of its sound. And when it is distorted by the wrong rhetoric in an attempt to "enrich it," it becomes impenetrable without gaining in power. English has to work to be elegant and simple, because its sounds are rarely if ever as spellbinding as Italian, and so much of its nature is tortuous. But how fabulous the honed expression of that tortuousness can be for a girl who sees so clearly reflected in this language her fervent and histrionic self: not one word to describe her feelings, but half a dozen variations. At sixteen, there was no contest. English was the language of my sensibility, the language with which I would write poems as full of words as Dylan Thomas's, novels as rich with emotion as *Villette*, dramas as powerful as Christopher Fry's *The Boy with a Cart*.

I ran away from Italian, carrying the parcel of intensity and aspiration, nourishing myself with the rich language of my parents, although I never consciously acknowledged then that it was my parents' language. I traveled with it for ten years, and ended up jettisoning the original aspiration: I no longer wanted to emulate Charlotte Brontë, Dylan Thomas or Christopher Fry. I did not even want to emulate Virginia Woolf or James

Joyce or Nabokov, nor even William Golding or Hopkins or T. S. Eliot. I ended up hitching rides of ambition here and there, but without a destination, homeless. Until I read Dino Buzzati's *Sessanta Racconti* and then Italo Calvino—*Il Barone Rampante, Il cavaliere dimezzato, Se una notte d'inverno,* and most especially *Fiabe Italiane.* Then my ambition became to write English with an Italian accent. In fact I wanted to write English with more than just an accent: my ambition became to throw out all that had first drawn me to English, all the baroque quality, and write English as if it were Italian. Now, while living in London, I could write my first volume of stories, *Rope-Dancer,* where most of the stories were inspired by Buzzati and Calvino. Now, while commuting to Southampton, I could write my first spare novel, *Concertina.* The two books were published concurrently a few months after my father's death in January 1985—less than a year after I sat beside him to watch *Una famiglia Americana in Italia,* when I found myself so shocked by the poverty of his spoken Italian. Had I come full circle?

No. The end of my father's life was the beginning of my life as a writer, and I was not in a circle or even a spiral, unless it be a twister. The role of Italian in all this turns out to be more complicated, even if I did physically move back to Perugia in 1986. I set myself up as a freelance writer, believed I could survive on an income patched together from writing and translations, supplemented by giving English lessons. But I had not come home as I thought when I made the move, and I had not found my style as I thought when I was composing my first works. English was playing its unfathomable role. Looking out at the brown-green Umbrian hills towards the ancient blue ridge of mountains, I dropped the Italian accent, abandoned the ambition to write

English as if it were Italian. My next novel, *The Placing of Kings,* was inspired by *Pride and Prejudice*—by the most English of English writers.

By the time I finished it, I knew that living in England was not living at home. But I also knew that if Italy was home, it was not providing me with a living, just as it had not provided generations of Italians with a living (albeit my kind of labor was not backbreaking physical labor), and I found myself taking on what would be perhaps the greatest challenge of all, by emigrating to America, to my father's Midwest. I had only been on the East Coast before, and no visit had lasted longer than the summer I spent with my father in 1984.

Now I watch myself trying to adapt to a world where the sense of history and of time are dizzyingly relative, a world where a European background and education are held in awe and despised at the same time, a world where Italian—my childhood language, the language with which I still add and subtract, the language of the only nursery rhymes I remember, the language of the only tongue twisters I can twist my tongue around—is *exotic.*

But is it in fact any more exotic than we must have seemed to Italians in 1957, when the documentary crew recorded our daily life in a small town that had rarely seen an American family living its daily life—a small town that had never seen a bunch of American kids speaking Italian as if it were their native tongue? Is this finally the circle I've been in all my life, this being perceived as "exotic," which pertains to anyone in any place who is not native of that place—whether it be an Italian or a Somali here in the States, an American or an Asian in Italy, an Asian or an Italian in Somalia? But unlike the Asian-American, the Somali-American, the Mexican-American, the Italo-American, I cannot enjoy the solidarity of belonging to a group, because I cannot say I am Italian here and I cannot say I am Italian in Italy. In fact, I cannot even say I am English here, or English in England. Nor can I say or think of myself as American, because I am not. I have to live straddling the three cultures I have absorbed. Yet in only one do I really feel at home.

This, I discover, is what I meant when I wrote that I feel as if I have never left Italy, in a way that parallels my father never having left Springfield, Illinois. The experience of childhood, which always determines *some* adult experience, for some determines *all* adult experience. However far my father went physically from that quiet, solitary, and thoughtful childhood steeped in American nineteenth-century culture, he was never willing or able to be free from it, and it informed all his adulthood, through every twist and change of twentieth-century intellectual life. I think that, however far I find myself from Italy, the country and the language will always determine all that I do.

Home remains the language I can no longer write as fluently as I write English, the Italian that now feels as clogged at the end of the pen as flour and water between the fingers—*impastata* is the only word, but useless because it communicates nothing to English readers who have not watched *contadine* prepare for a wedding feast by making fresh pasta and *gnocchi,* and cannot see the laboring and chapped hands placing some of the mixture in front of me, and cannot feel the exact stickiness the word conveys.

Home is the words: the word *limpido,* for example, that does not limp as "limpid" does when denied the strong accent of the final *o*, but somehow contains in full the transparency of air on autumn days after the first violent sea storms of the year had exhausted themselves against the poor jagged cliffs, just in time for the picking of the last grapes. The sky would turn *azzurro* once more, in time for the final nets to be put down under the olive trees; at the next storm, all the olives would be shaken from the trees clinging to the steep terraced hill and roll down the slopes. Perhaps a landslide—how much more frightening the words *frana* and *valanga* are—would cut a deep slice off the outer edge of the already narrow road winding down into Levanto from the house, and up and around to Bonassola.

Home is the word *incendio*, containing so much more than "a fire" ever could: the sight of the forest on the other side of the bay, on the mountain between Levanto and Monterosso, ablaze, fire rising high in the ink-black sky, a stippling of stars with orange sparks. The sounds, not of sirens, but of church bells ringing, and human voices calling and echoing, and behind those sounds the crackle of wood in flames; the smell of smoke drifting for days, for weeks across the bay to our house. Every time we looked across, the mountain lay bald and exposed. Only long after we had left did the low scrub appear, and only now, forty-five years later, are the small portions that have not been built up green with young oak-sapling and walnut trees once more.

Home is the word *papavero*, poppy, that conjures up with such clarity the song that was sung in those years, in fields where the flower gloried among the ticklish hay, *Lo sai che i papaveri son alti alti alti e tu sei piccolina, lo sai che i papaveri son alti alti, sei nata paperina che cosa ci vuoi far,* and trails in its wake the other song, *Aveva una casetta piccolina in Canadà, con vasche pesciolini e tanti fiori di lillà, e tutte le ragazze che passavano di la dicevano che bella la casetta in Canadà.* These songs were never heard on the radio, but always in those fields, always to the accompaniment of the accordion and sometimes the harmonica, instruments only the men played. Is it one long summer picnic forever imprinted on my memory, or was it a series of outings with Maria and Alice and their village boyfriends? I cannot remember the details, but the songs and the words unlock the smell of the hay, the taunts and the teases of endless hot afternoons, and the playing, singing, and dancing which started as soon as the heat abated and continued by the light of paraffin-filled rags wrapped around thick sticks and made into torches. No words in English have this power, to take me back home to childhood.

# Personal and Singular

## Ha-yun Jung

In Korean, the first-person singular is an elusive voice. The simple English sentence "I want an apple" sounds awkward when translated, word for word, into Korean. A Korean person is much more likely to say something that could be translated as "It would be nice to have an apple." Omitting "I" is never a grammatical defect; on the contrary, the sentence sounds more polished without it. Rarely will you hear a Korean speak—or write—consecutive sentences that start with I-this, I-that. "I" seems content to crawl behind the curtain at the first given moment.

And when it comes to possessive forms, "our" is often used in the place of "my." "My country," "my people," "my neighborhood" are all very unusual expressions in Korean, even when one is speaking as an individual. This is all the more evident when referring to family members; even when the speaker is an only child, one will say "our" mother or father, never "my."

I (there's that "I"!) am a single parent, but when I speak Korean I say "our son." And in English I am prone to saying things like "So then we had to go fill out a prescription for our kid" to a casual acquaintance I might see while in line at Starbucks. Then I quickly realize, from the slightly confused look on the person's face, that to the American ear what I said sounds like a slip. "Poor thing. After four years, she still hasn't gotten over her divorce," my listener probably concludes.

I used to have a sibling, but I no longer do; yet I refer to my mother as "our mom" in Korean, just as my deceased father is still "our dad." And my brother, dead or alive, will always be *uri dongsaeng*, "our little brother."

Perhaps this is why I write in English, and not in the language that I was born into.


Our family arrived in Bangkok, Thailand, in 1975. A bitter winter chill had seen us off in Seoul, the city I had lived in all nine-and-a-half years of my life, but as soon as we stepped out of the airport terminal the humid heat of this new land filled my nostrils. My brother, two years younger than I, frowned at the glare of the sun. His eyes were too sensitive. But I lifted my face and greeted the light, felt the warmth spread all over. It really was summer here in the middle of November, just as my parents had explained, with fascination.

And it would be summer, sweltering summer, all year long, all through the three years of our stay. These years would remain in my memory as a single season made up of nothing but sun and rain, which made everything around me grow; the grass, the insects, the opulent orchids, the sky-high coconut trees, the fiery red salamanders that lurked under bushes like fat lumps of lust. And this was where I would grow, in surprising spurts, into an unfamiliar female body.

We moved into a gated housing complex designed for expatriate families, with landscaped lawns and tennis courts and a maid quarter—a narrow block of bare cement walls and floors and a wash room with only a tap—attached to every unit. Despite the new and exotic setting, at first this protected world did not appear so different from our old neighborhood in Seoul. We had lived in a Japanese colonial-style house nestled in a winding web of hilly roads, only doors away from our grandparents and uncles and aunts, surrounded by servants and drivers, locked inside a set of reliable routines and rituals. Our lives, it seemed, would go on the same way, whether we were back home or on the other side of the South China Sea.

My brother and I had grown up listening to accounts of our parents' wedding. It had taken place at the height of both our grandfathers' careers, attended by the Prime Minister and other dignitaries, allegedly causing a traffic jam downtown. My mother's father was the founder and principal of the prestigious Seoul High School, which he envisioned as the Korean version of Eton. My father had been one of his students, one of the many boys—"All of them," as my mother still claims—who had competed for the attention of the five beautiful daughters at the principal's on-campus residence. By the time they got married, my father and mother were graduates of top universities, and my paternal grandfather, a revered lawyer, had entered a political career as the face of integrity in the Park Chung Hee military regime's ruling party. Ever since I can remember, my brother and I were constantly being referred to as so-and-so's grandchildren, and we believed this was a blessing that would see us through in life, that our place in the world had already been shaped for us.

In Bangkok, my father, in his mid-thirties, was the commercial attaché for the South Korean embassy, headed for a future in public office. My mother was his pretty, petite wife, an English Literature major who cooked and sewed and read Dr. Spock, who, upon arriving in this new country, eagerly ventured into attending antique auctions and bridge games and shopping at Jim Thompson.

English was the language spoken at Ruamrudee International School, an institution founded by Redemptorist fathers, whose name meant "union of hearts" in Thai. The Bangkok expatriate community was huge, and the Americans had their own school, as did the British, the French, and the Japanese. As a result, the student population at Ruamrudee was truly international, with a Third World focus: a majority of rich Thai and Chinese kids, plus Indian, Filipino, Scandinavian, and even a scattered few from the Eastern bloc. Coming from the fanatical anti-Communist society of the Park Chung Hee era, I remember being at a complete loss as to how I was going to look at or talk to Nikola, a classmate with wide brown eyes and soft curls who was the son of a Romanian diplomat.

The school, a concrete cube of a building with a bare cement courtyard, was actually a mere annex to the Holy Redeemer Church that dominated the grounds. The huge white cathedral had a grand, slanted roof, tiled in blue and red and lots of gold, identical to those of the royal palaces and Buddhist temples all around Bangkok. Yet it was a church, with crosses and stained glass and figures of Jesus Christ. Its facade was lined with a long row of doors that led straight into the pews. These doors were always open, with cool winds blowing through them, in and out, no matter how scorching the weather. It was an alien mystery to me, just like the children at school who looked so different from the people back in Korea. These kids made me feel unremarkable and bland, with their pierced ears, hairy arms, gold chains, oily smells and all sorts of head wraps, from turbans to fist-sized knots that sat on the heads of long-lashed, round-eyed Sikh boys.

There were no American students at Ruamrudee, but our curriculum was American, as were our principal, Mr. Maxwell (who had a buttery roar of a voice and a balloon-like belly that hung over his belt), and the fathers and sisters who led the Lord's Prayer during assembly, following the raising of the Thai flag. We learned about the fifty states and their capitals, about Lewis and Clark and Paul Revere, though most of us had never been to the United States. In music class, our Filipino teacher taught us to sing "John Henry," "My Favorite Things" and "America the Beautiful."

My lessons in English began with picture books showing a word for every letter of the alphabet. At age nine, I could absorb without complication what words meant and how sentences were structured, but learning how to pronounce these unfamiliar vowels and consonants took much conscious effort. Korean is phonetically a far less flamboyant language than English; it almost sounds monotonous in comparison, each syllable of a word uttered in equal length and stress. The *f, r, v, z* and *th* sounds are all non-existent in Korean and I would have to tighten my tummy, strain my throat, and purse my lips, trying to figure out exactly how to roll and twist and keep afloat my tongue. It felt like an extremely secretive, personal effort, all taking place deep inside of my mouth. "U is for um-brel-la—" I would try to read out loud, reminding myself of the difference between the *r* and the *l* sounds; then I would try to figure out the stress and completely go blank—*How did that go again? How do you make your mouth spit out all those sounds at the rush of the second syllable? I sound like I am about to throw up!* At assembly every morning I stood in the sun-soaked courtyard, my feet already sweaty inside thick white socks, and listened for the smooth, effortless twang in Mr. Maxwell's every word— "A-a-n an-nou-ncement from the high school da-a-nce commit-tee . . ."—then tried to join everyone in prayer, bringing my hands together, closing my eyes, mouthing the words to practice my pronunciation, though I had no idea what they meant or who and where "our father" was.

The rest of this country, beyond our home, school and depart-ment stores, my brother and I saw only from inside of our air-conditioned, chauffeur-driven Volvo with the diplomatic plates. On our way to and back from school, we passed several market-places filled with fume and clutter, streets overflowing with three-wheeled *tuk-tuks*, trucks decorated with paintings of women in bikinis, packed buses rattling along with passengers dangling in the doorway, tilting the vehicle. Local kids, skinny and shrill-voiced, blocked the cars at every red light, peddling orchid gar-lands, offering to clean the windshield, begging for coins. When we rolled down the car window for only a short moment, the steamy odor of the outside world rushed in—a pungent mix of *phakchi* and jasmine rice, sweat and smoke, sweet mango and slow-burning incense. The whole and skinned poultry that hung upside down from hooks outside the storefronts looked grue-some, but their meaty aroma made my mouth water. My mother never let us buy food from the street. She claimed it was unreli-able, especially for my brother, who got rashes from shellfish and fell sick from MSG at restaurants. There seemed to be danger and death on these streets, but at the same time the bustle was bursting with life, like luscious blossoms sprouting after the monsoon.

Not long after arriving in Bangkok, I began having repeating nightmares. In the middle of the night, I would wake up crying, waving my arms and legs, struggling to pull away the swarm of worms and caterpillars and snakes crawling all over my body. My bed was overflowing with them, and the more I tried to get away, the deeper I would sink. Even when I opened my eyes, the sweat on my skin felt slimy, like those slithery, faceless creatures. These nights, dark and dank like a deep hole, had to be battled by myself. No one else noticed. And in the morning, as my brother and I headed out into the city, I saw dead frogs on the driveway, squashed flat on the asphalt by late returning cars, already dry and shapeless in the scalding sun, thin as paper cutouts.


Towards the end of his life, my father would cringe and curse when he talked about Thailand. "The heat, that is what made me ill," he said.

The liver does not reveal its ailments through pain; instead, it takes away pleasures—of the senses, of physical energy, of simple optimism. Hepatitis robbed my father of the ability to enjoy taste and he spent decades talking about food with desperate nostalgia. He could never appreciate Thai cuisine; he had believed at first—before he was diagnosed—that his health was deteriorating because of the overwhelming unfamiliarity of this new food. Just the thought of fish sauce, lemongrass, coconut milk and long grain rice would later make him nauseous, bringing back early physical memories of a disease that would eventually kill him, gradually hardening his liver into an ugly yellow block, the color of a stinky, overripe durian.

Over our first summer break in Bangkok, my father began coming home for lunch and a nap, then reluctantly returning to the embassy when the mid-day sizzle had subsided, if only slightly. When this didn't help, he figured the lethargy was due to a lack of exercise and shot hoops under the sun before his nap and played more golf on weekends. "It was practically suicide," he would say years later, "clueless that I was helping sick cells multiply themselves, inviting them to take over my body."

When a new Korean ambassador arrived the following year, my father had been through several leaves and a month-long stay in the hospital. He did not want to attend the ambassador's first family luncheon—he rarely got out of bed on Sundays—but he had no choice.

The residence was a modern house with wide, white rooms and long panels of glass that looked out into a garden, a pool, and an atrium displaying strangely twisted rocks as if they were art. I was now one of the older kids in the group. Two other girls and I were exploring the rooms, crossing the vast emptiness of each, wondering what all these rooms were for. We came across a long, high-ceilinged marble hallway, where we found a group of boys pointing and laughing at something, at someone. It was my father, seated in an armchair placed against a tall wall, his elbows on the arm rests, his hands clasped in front of him, his head dipped as if in a low bow, his expression so solemn and somber that you would think he was praying. But he was asleep. He could not make it through the day without a nap and I knew it, but I wanted to slap him awake. Behind him hung a huge painting of nothing, made up entirely of different shades of blue. He looked utterly isolated, unable to keep up with the others, unaware of the ridicule, barely holding himself together in that small corner. My brother followed other boys into the hallway and joined in the laughter; I could not tell if he knew what was going on. I turned away, as if this man had nothing to do with me.

My brother and I did not fly back to Korea for our grandfather's funeral. We still had a month to go until vacation—I was in fifth grade and my brother in third—so we dutifully attended school, doing our homework, watching "Six Million Dollar Man" and "Charlie's Angels" while our maid Wong served us grilled cheese sandwiches or bowls of Ichiban ramen.

"There would be too much going on," our mother told us, when we demanded their reason for leaving us behind. My brother and I could not see, at least not then, what our grandfather's death meant and might do to the family. My father's father was 84 years old when he died, a paterfamilias who had under his wing a family of almost thirty, including his two wives, two brothers, thirteen children, and the widows, widowers, and offspring left behind by the four sons and two daughters that he had lost during the Korean War. Five years before his death, he had taken an unexpected turn towards political dissent, when he openly declared, as chairman of the ruling party, that he would vote against President Park Chung Hee's constitution reforms, a move that would ensure Park's third—then fourth and fifth—term in office. The law was passed, of course, and our grandfather won quiet respect but also faced persecution. When he died, he did not have much to leave behind but the overbearing burden of his legend.

Much later, after our family returned to Korea that year, my brother and I were shown a silent home movie of the funeral. We sat in the study that our grandfather had occupied for decades, once stacked with dusty old books and decorated with stoic calligraphy. Now its walls were covered with cheap wallpaper too thin to mask the old stains and the bookshelves were scattered with mahjong pieces and Johnnie Walker bottles. The room had been taken over by my father's older brother, who would in a few years go bankrupt and lose everything, including the old house. In the movie, I saw everyone in our extended family—the women in traditional white cotton *hanbok,* the men in black suits and conical mourners' hats—weeping, as if they were in fear, as if the funeral would not be the end but the beginning of something terrifying. My father's face looked crumbled, as if his eyes and nose and lips had been rearranged. I stared at him on the screen, astounded at the unfamiliarity, and though there was no sound, I slowly realized that he was wailing, like an animal in pain. It was the first time I had seen him cry.

It was while we were by ourselves in Bangkok, our parents still away in Seoul, that Mrs. Shanti died. She was from India and taught high school, wore beautiful saris of bold colors and a thick pile of thin, shiny bracelets that chimed when she walked by. I remember seeing her at the cafeteria only several days before we heard the news, the dark make-up on her eyes glamorous as always, her strides sure but light, as if she were gliding an inch above the ground. It was a stroke that took her.

The entire school was sent to pay respects to Mrs. Shanti at the cathedral. All the classes lined up along the aisle, proceeding toward the altar. I had no idea what to expect once I got there. The morning sun glazed the doorways along both sides of the nave with white, foamy light. I had never been in here. It was not as dark as I had imagined, but the air was dense and damp, as if I could feel the silent chill dripping in long, heavy drops, landing on my forehead, on my bare arms, down the back of my neck. When the wind blew in from the outside, it carried with it faint remnants of the greasy heat that was starting to boil up.

There I stood, in front of the altar, next to a casket placed at an angle to its left. Mrs. Shanti lay in white satin, dressed in a stiff new sari, her face as purple as her blouse, white, puffy cotton balls pushed deep into her nostrils. I imagined the dead Mrs. Shanti dressing herself for one last time, putting on her jewelry and her lipstick, pulling up her hair in a smooth chignon, then lying back inside her coffin, closing her eyes, giving in with a stale sigh. She looked alive, yet the decay was so palpable it made me nauseous. I wondered if my grandfather looked like this, buried under the ground, the traditional grave mound— still only a fresh, bald pile of earth—pressing down on him. I drew a cross on my chest, not knowing what else to do, and walked back into the daylight that blinded my eyes.

That year, I got my period and grew so much that by the time I got to sixth grade I was the tallest in my class. I let my hair grow, and the tomboyish bob cut that my mom had always insisted on quickly dissolved into thick, untamable abundance.

I was now allowed to go to parties, though only during the day, often taking a cab on my own. The girls in my class talked endlessly about our first school dance, coming up around Christmas, but by then I would have left the country. The last party I went to was a birthday bash for Marissa, a Filipino friend, at her mansion-like home with an overgrown garden. She had many older siblings and their friends had been invited as well. To my dismay, Chi-wen, an eighth-grader from Taiwan, with his wobbly Mandarin accent and uncool no-brand tennis shoes, kept making eye contact. I felt lithe and light—which was rare, after all that growing—in my faded jeans and gauzy white peasant blouse.

As the late afternoon heat simmered down, we moved outside, bored with not having much to do but sip Fanta and listen to Boney M and play Monopoly. The garden was shady under the looming trees and I lingered at the edge of the patio, hesitating to step onto the thick grass.

"A snake!" someone called out, pointing to the shade of a banana tree, draped with huge paddle-shaped leaves, bearing bubbly clusters of new fruit.

I could not see the snake, but it seemed as if the entire garden was moving, overflowing with batches of fleshy leaves, fresh green coils stretching from vines, carnivorous-looking flowers with petals like perked-up lips. I could not move. Just as in my dreams, I felt as if I were drowning in a pool of snakes, wrapping around my limbs and pulling me down.

Other kids gathered in front of the tree and joined in as the high school boys began to throw rocks, some striking at the target with a stick. Everyone was evidently having fun, the girls' squeals breaking into laughter, the boys cheering, as if this had been planned as part of the festivity all along. Then, finally someone called out, "I got it!" It was Chi-wen, holding up the black serpent, shiny and sinuous. He looked over at me with a happy, harmless grin. I kicked at my feet, stumbling to turn around, and pushed myself out the gate, panting all the way down the alley to the busy street. I stopped the first cab I saw. As I slammed the creaky backseat door, Chi-wen tapped the roof of the car, out of breath.

"You okay?" he asked.

"That was so gross," I said, exaggerating my *o*'s.

"Sorry, sorry." He held up his arms, to show he no longer had the dead snake.

"Soi Srinakorn, fifteen *baht*?" I said to the cab driver, negotiating the fare with the few Thai words I could handle, lengthening the vowels and rolling the *r*'s, declaring, *I am an English-speaking foreigner.* "Bye," I said to Chi-wen and as the taxi pulled away, I felt a hot rush of anticipation, leaving him standing there, flushed and forlorn.

When we returned to Korea in November of 1978, we were greeted by the first cold we experienced in three years—biting, harsh and oppressive. It was the same month that we left, but this time the winter air felt so strange I was scared to breathe. My toes would go numb in my sneakers when I was outside and I could not smell anything, as if there were no room in this frozen air for smells to move around.

Almost everyone we knew had now moved to high-rise apartments that had started to go up all around southern Seoul, the new, modern half of the 500-year-old capital. Our parents moved us into a three-bedroom unit in Banpo, an entire neighborhood built around two hundred identical gray buildings. The four of us lived on the first floor of Bldg. #56 for thirteen years, trapped inside that rectangular cell, divided into smaller squares sealed from the outside world like air-tight containers. In my memory, that apartment is always brown, with the drapes drawn; always tidy, everything in its place, because things were seldom moved, like the silver wine goblets with elephant engravings that my mother had brought back from Thailand. They sat on the kitchen cabinet shelf for years and years, turning black like cavities.

My first day at Sehwa Girls' Junior High was in March. We had been back in Seoul for three months, but it was still cold and I was uncomfortable under the layers of bulky thermal underwear and ill-fitting uniform, a spartan black jacket and skirt. My eyes were puffy from crying all night, after getting my hair cut to the required one-centimeter-below-the-ears length. I sat in the classroom with seventy other girls, all wearing the exact same clothes and shoes, with the exact same hair, parted and pinned to one side, the backs of our necks shaved blue with electric hair clippers. A stern portrait of President Park Chung Hee hung above the blackboard next to Taegeuk-ki, the national flag.

Every morning at the school gate, the senior student inspectors checked our hair and uniforms as we bowed. And every morning I would feel like someone was going to see through me, despite my perfect get-up, and pull me out of the orderly procession to interrogate: *Why don't you look like all the others? Why don't you fit in?*

The Korean that I reencountered in Seoul was a language of hierarchy, of honorifics and humble submission. Because I was no longer the content, innocent nine-year-old, the intimate way that I used to talk was not of much use. I had to constantly remind myself of my relation with the person I was speaking to, for it dictated every single pronoun and verb form I was to utter. And I began to learn, instinctively, what was speakable and unspeakable. When a teacher scolded you, the only way to respond was, "It was my fault." Trying to explain was considered talking back. In Korean, I did not know how to speak of everything I missed about Bangkok—the heat, the colors, the dance I never got to attend, the way Chi-wen had looked at me in that lush garden.

At the same time, my English lessons at school retreated to the alphabet, see-saw-seen, I-we/you-you/he-she-they, *What is your name?*

Our family had come back to the place where we used to live but it seemed that we had accidentally stepped into another life. Everything changed. To follow in his late father's footsteps, my father quit the ministry and ran for a seat in the National Assembly, but failed. He never would regain the old glory; instead he lost his money, his health and his bond with the rest of his family. My mother began to go through long periods of depression, which would slowly progress into bouts of frenzied hope, only to crash back down. She was diagnosed with bipolar disorder and there were many afternoons when I came home from school to find out that she had again been hospitalized. It would take weeks, sometimes months, until she came home again, with shaking fingers and slurred speech and unkempt hair.

We were no longer "us." My brother and I went about doing what we had to in order to grow up, but separately, alone behind the doors of our rooms.

I started to keep a diary in English. I no longer used English with other people; it had become a language that was completely personal and singularly mine. Recently I dug out the old, yellowed notebook from a box that I have carried with me across states and countries and continents. What amazed me was that my writing was entirely devoid of descriptions or details, with hardly a mention of friends or family, filled with sentences that began with "I," relentlessly pouring out how *I* felt, over and over, as if the words were coming from solely within myself, a place disconnected with the outside world, a place where no one or nothing else could find a way in.

On Sept. 25th, 1981, the day I woke to find my mother unconscious, with a bottle of rat poison by her bedside, I came home from the hospital, closed the door, sat at my desk and wrote, in English: "I don't know where to begin. I can't believe it."

My mother would live on, through more suicide attempts and manic sprees, through the deaths of others.

Three weeks before the second-year memorial service for our father, my brother, who had been missing for over a month, was found in his car, frozen dead stiff at 28, in a parking lot by the Han River, a short ten-minute drive on the riverside expressway from the Banpo apartment, where our mother had been waiting and waiting. That night in Boston, I got on a plane that would take me back to Seoul, flying over the white glaciers of Alaska, where there was no summer. I was four months pregnant.

And I live on, not feeling whole in Korean or in English. For me, one language is complementary to the other, one always lacking a capacity that the other has. And I have a fear, constantly, of not quite being understood in just one language: *Do you know what I am trying to say? Do you know who I am?*

POLISH

# On Being an Orphaned Writer

## Louis Begley

In the late summer of 2002, I completed the draft of a new
novel, *Shipwreck*. Publishing house gears grind slowly when
they process fiction that is not expected to bring down a shower
of gold, so that I received my editor's comments only a short
while before the Christmas vacation. I made the final revisions
during that two-week period and countless hours I later stole
from my work as a lawyer. Only one of my editor's suggestions
concerned structure. It was easy to handle. The rest were the
sort of take it or leave it pencil notations—some of them extraor-
dinarily helpful—that a gifted reader cannot resist making on
the margins of a manuscript. Nevertheless, dealing with these
pencil squiggles took an extraordinary amount of time, and left
me even more despondent and apprehensive than is usual in
that desolate time of the year. My spirits did lift when I finally
read the retyped novel. Once again, I began to think that what I
had written was comely. But I knew that it would take very little
to shatter my calm, perhaps nothing more than the need to
reread in order to repair foolish inconsistencies in the plot or the
time line that the copy editor, who has worked on all my novels,
will track down with her unfailing instincts of a bounty hunter. I
know the reasons for my slowness and uncertainty, and I don't

confuse them with the doubts that assail every novelist when he delivers a finished manuscript to his publisher—an act in its way as grave as giving up a child for adoption. Until that moment you had in your possession a sheaf of pages with which you communed daily, devoting to them non-stop thought and care. Suddenly, it's adieu forever: the book will pass into the hands of strangers, and who is to say how they will treat it? Will it meet indifference or hostility or favor, will it be understood? All you can do is wish it luck. Sometimes you think you would rather stand naked among the noontime crowd in Times Square than witness your book's ordeal.

The soil in which my special anxieties are rooted is the precarious relationship between me and the English language. The circumstances are as follows: Polish is my mother tongue. Since by reason of events over which I had no control I write instead in English, I am an orphaned writer. English is not even my first or second language; I did not begin to learn it until I was eleven or twelve, in preparation for leaving Poland. That is where I was born almost seventy years ago, and where I lived until early October of 1946, around the time of my thirteenth birthday. The next stop was France. But my parents and I remained in Paris only for a few months; we left for New York at the end of February 1947. Despite many absences, some of which were relatively long—when I was away at college and law school, during my military service in the U.S. Army in Germany, and in the years when I worked at my law firm's office in Paris—New York has been my home ever since.

I did not return to Poland until 1994, when I went to Warsaw on legal business. Several visits to Warsaw followed, all quite short, and only one of them, in 1995, I made as a writer. The reason was the publication, in Polish translation, of my first novel, *Wartime Lies*, which had appeared in the original English in 1991. In it I recount the life in Poland, during World War II, of a Polish Jewish boy, whom I call Maciek, and his aunt; in a number of respects, although my novel is in no sense an autobiography, Maciek's adventures resemble my own. This is especially true of the boy's chaotic and inadequate education. Before I arrived in New York, my schooling had consisted of nothing more than sporadic lessons in Warsaw during the War from a memorable tutor who risked her life to give them, whatever my mother managed to teach me, and one year, directly after the War ended, at a *gimnazjum* in Cracow. Naturally, all of this was in Polish, which my parents and I, just like Maciek and his aunt, spoke to each other. The only foreign language I learned during the War was German. Now my German is mostly dormant; it stirs when I urgently need it. Sometime in the interval between the Soviet occupation in September 1939 of Eastern Poland, where my parents and I then lived, and Germany's breach of the Ribbentrop-Molotov Pact in 1941, whereupon the Wehrmacht drove away the Soviet troops and commenced its thrust into Russian territory, I also studied Russian. I have forgotten it completely. Learning French came later. Paradoxically, that is a language in which I am completely at ease. I always speak it with my wife, it being her native tongue and the language of our courtship.

And Polish? My connection with it has remained unbroken. I still use it in conversations with my mother and her Polish housekeeper, and the occasional Poles I encounter in New York. When I was in Warsaw, it never occurred to me to speak English or French to the many Poles who are fluent in those languages. It was natural to use Polish. It is a rare night when I do not have nightmares about World War II in Poland; they are invariably in Polish. When I do sums in my head, or count wine glasses set out on the sideboard for a cocktail party we are about to give, I begin in Polish, and switch to English only after I have become conscious of the absurdity of what I am doing. The songs I sing off key in the car to fight against drowsiness are as often as not Polish folksongs and military airs I learned as a child; I still remember hundreds of lines of Polish poems my mother required me to memorize. Only the other week, I received a remarkable letter in Polish from an eleven-year-old schoolgirl living in Warsaw, provoked by her having read *Wartime Lies* with her grandfather and having been to see Roman Polanski's film *The Pianist*. She put some hard questions about the cruelty portrayed in both works and expressed the hope that I would answer in Polish, if I still remembered it. I composed the reply immediately and asked a Polish friend to correct gross mistakes. He told me there weren't any. Omissions of letters and words abounded, just as they do in my English texts, in part because I think faster than I write in longhand or type. Of course, I have never stopped reading Polish novels and Polish poetry. Thus, among the most moving literary discoveries I have made in the last two decades have been the Polish poet Zbigniew Herbert and the Polish novelist and playwright Witold Gombrowicz, who stand at the pinnacle of twentieth-century literature. Close after Gombrowicz, and of the same generation as Herbert, comes the short story writer and essayist Gustaw Herling-Grudzinski. I came upon his work reviewing a collection of his short stories. He too has his place in my pantheon.

Sometimes cultural change turns out to be far slower than one would expect. After a reading I gave in Warsaw in 1995, from *Wartime Lies,* someone in the audience asked me to say any poem I had learned as a child. Without a moment's thought, laughing with pleasure, I launched into lines about a railroad car full of grotesquely fat men eating fat (and delicious) sausages, Polish *kielbasy.* This charming poem, by Julian Tuwim, the greatest of Polish poets active between the two World Wars, was one that every Polish child of my generation with more or less educated parents knew by heart and loved. As I recited it, though, my exhilaration gave way to sadness and fear that this fragment of pre-War Poland so vivid in my memory would seem alien, and perhaps ludicrous, to a roomful of post–Cold War Poles. My astonishment and joy were extreme when I heard the audience speaking the lines in unison with me. My past was alive in their present.

A curious reader might ask about my English. Of course, it is very good. All my education was in the United States, after I left Poland. By the time I was a high school senior, in 1949, I wrote English well enough to win a city-wide short story contest administered by New York University. The prize was a leather-bound volume of the Oxford Book of English Poetry, which in due course I gave to my older son, a lover of literature who drowned it in the bathtub in which he was soaking. I was an English major in college, and composed short stories for the sort of creative writing courses one took until, in the spring of my junior year, I decided I had better stop because I had nothing to say. It would be more precise and less coy to admit that there was nothing that I was ready to write and stand by as my truth. Afterward, I became engaged in the kind of law practice that requires one to produce, as the major part of one's work, letters of advice, memoranda of law, contracts and briefs, advancement in the profession depending largely on the view one's elders took of the quality of the writing. It was therefore not wholly accurate to think of me as a novice when, in 1989, at the age of fifty-six, I completed my first novel. I had in reality been honing my skills relentlessly, although not in the conventional manner. Even more important for the development of English as my best language, and the only language in which I want to write works of imagination, was serving in the U.S. Army as an enlisted man and having three American children, two of them born before I was thirty and the third only two months after my thirtieth birthday. G.I. talk and the language of the nursery and playground games: had I not experienced them fully, my written English, however literary and elegant I might make it, would be like a dressed-up corpse.

Even though I am told that my writing does not show signs of *rigor mortis,* it is a fact that I write slowly and laboriously, pausing after every word I set down. I change it countless times and repeat the process with each sentence and paragraph before I can move forward. The vision of Trollope composing the Barchester novels in a railroad car, traveling desk balanced on his knees, with hardly an erasure or addition needed before the manuscript went off to the publisher, fills me with admiration, envy, and dull despair. I too can perform on the high wire when I write a legal text or an essay; writing fiction I need to keep my feet on the ground. Perfectionism and perennial dissatisfaction with everything I do are not alone to blame: it seems to me that when I write in English I lack normal spontaneity, let alone the unbeatable self-assurance a writer needs to soar or to be outrageous. I know that I do manage from time to time to be outrageous in my fiction, but the stress falls on the verb "manage."

Nothing about those effects is instant. The truth is that even today, after an immersion of more than fifty-five years in the English language, I am never completely confident that I have gotten right whatever it is that I write down, certainly not on the first try. Knowing objectively that often—perhaps most often—in fact I do, is not a consolation. In that respect only, I am not unlike my great countryman, Joseph Conrad. But Conrad had more of an excuse: he began to learn English only at the age of twenty-one; he was thirty-eight when his first novel, *Almayer's Folly,* was published, and he had spent most of the intervening years on the high seas. Vladimir Nabokov's command of the English language is a different case altogether. English was in effect Nabokov's first language: he learned to read it before he could read Russian. Becoming thoroughly proficient in a "civilized" tongue, usually the French, and leaving the vernacular for later, to be absorbed as a part of growing up, was usual in the nineteenth century among Slavic upper-class families. There was a series of English and French governesses who took care of the Nabokov children, and it wasn't until Vladimir was seven that his father, alarmed by his sons' backwardness in their native language, engaged the schoolmaster from the village adjoining the family estate to teach them to read and write in Russian.

To go back to the torment I experienced revising the manuscript of my most recent novel, its immediate cause was the number of times my editor was in essence questioning my diction, the correctness of the way I expressed myself in English. It didn't matter that he wasn't always right. What hurt was the contrast between his instinctive grasp of how one would normally say whatever it was that I wanted to express and my doubts: my need to grope to find the way, to test each sentence by reading it aloud. He had kept his birthright—the ability to use his mother tongue in his calling—and I had lost mine. Whether I would have had the spontaneity and freedom that I feel I lack as a novelist writing in English, a language I didn't master until I was fourteen, if I had become a novelist writing in my native Polish, is an intriguing question to which obviously there is no reliable answer. I think, though, that my love for the Polish language, and the way in which it has remained present in my conscious and subconscious memory, are favorable indications.

An even more difficult question is whether I would have become a writer of fiction at all if my parents had not, driven by the need to escape from the ghosts of so many of our unburied dead and the oppressive weight of Stalinism, left Poland with me in 1946, as soon as they had acquired the means to do so—if they had not chosen the adventure of penniless emigration over the comfort, however precarious, of remaining in Cracow. I do not believe that a novelist's talent is one of those that bear fruit regardless of circumstances, being probably different in this regard from the gift for music or the sciences, and, for that matter, certain kinds of physical prowess. I am convinced that my having become able, rather late in life, to write fiction was the result of the peace I finally made with the past and its effect on my identity. But important aspects of that past—the extermination of Polish Jews by Germans during World War II, and the attitude of the vast majority of non-Jewish Poles toward the abject humiliation and then slaughter of some three million of their Jewish fellow citizens—were taboo as subjects for open discussion in post-War Poland under the Communist regime. They remained such even after the advent of Solidarity and well into the 1990s. Indeed, the taboo may not have been fully lifted until the revelations in 2001 by the historian Jan T. Gross in his book *Neighbors: The Destruction of the Jewish Community in Jedwabne, Poland,* concerning the pogrom in 1941 in the very small town of Jedwabne, in the course of which half of its population, some 1,600 Jews, were savagely murdered by the other (Catholic) half. The publication of Gross's book was followed by a fierce debate in Poland that brought many issues into the open and disposed of many myths. In the conditions that prevailed in Poland after the War ended, a not inconsiderable number of Jews who survived in Poland and did not leave, and of Jews who returned to Poland or were born there after the War, including some who gained prominence in public life, were careful not to let their being of Jewish birth or faith be evident, in any event not to be evident enough to expose them to more or less attenuated forms of harassment or to put their careers at risk. The analogy to how, under German occupation, my mother and I, and many of those same Polish Jews and their parents, avoided the ghetto and extermination by passing for Catholic Poles, is painful. I cannot believe that in those conditions such literary talent as I have would have led me to write novels; it might have developed in other directions or not have progressed beyond sustaining my love for books and language. In fact, I am not aware of any Polish Jews of my generation or younger writing novels or poetry in Polish, perhaps there are some who are not well known, or whose being Jewish simply has not come to my attention. The contrast is striking when one looks at the generations of Polish Jews that came to maturity in Poland between the two World Wars, out of which came many major figures in Polish literature, among them Julian Tuwim and Herling-Grudzinski, whom I have already mentioned, and Josef Wittlin.

The literary silence of Polish Jews living in Poland since World War II may be of no significance: there is no orderly progress based on nationality in the production of writers, and whether writers are Jews or not is not of significance except when they use in their work specifically Jewish material to which the accident of upbringing gave them special access. In my own case, I wrote my first novel on the quintessentially Jewish subject of survival during the War, because it was an experience that had seared me. I must have felt that to write about other subjects and to remain silent about the War in Poland was impossible; perhaps it was even dishonorable. That task completed, I have had no further interest in Jewish or Polish material. To the contrary, I have dealt in novel after novel with great human themes that are not limited by national, religious or, for that matter, social boundaries: the effect on us of losing those we love the most; our profound and total loneliness, from which only the power of Eros liberates us; the randomness of the catastrophes that befall us; and the hash we make of relationships that count for us the most. My settings have been those that I thought suited best the story I was going to tell, and that I know sufficiently. Thus my characters have found themselves on the east coast of the United States, in France and Italy, on a Greek island, in Brazil, and in Tokyo and Beijing.

Nevertheless, I have never been free of the pull of Poland. Or is it in reality the pull of the Polish language and Polish literature? This is a question I have put to myself more than once, reflecting on how I constructed the setting of the story I told in *Wartime Lies*. My first novel was a work of fiction based in part on recollections of what happened to me and, in at least equal part, on stories I heard during the War and soon afterward about the misadventures of others. Writing it, I soon realized that I had forgotten the topography of every place I had known in Poland, except the town where I was born, and that even that memory had been stripped down by time to a few startling essentials. Therefore, when I constructed the itineraries of the little boy and his aunt, to find my way I had to pore over the street maps of Lwów and Warsaw. I remembered best the interiors, for the simple reason that avoiding denunciation and capture made it preferable to go out into the city as little as might be thought appropriate for a young woman and a little boy leading an ostensibly normal life. There were as well, alas, certain outdoor scenes in my novel the visual memory of which is etched in my skin like the message that the great harrow wrote with acid on the back of the prisoner in Kafka's "In the Penal Colony."

One of the very happy memories I had been able to retain—I did not use it in *Wartime Lies* because for a number of reasons it did not fit—was of a visit to my grandparents' small property in a remote Polish countryside. I discovered, however, thinking intensively about the image in my mind of the low, weatherbeaten wood house, a connection between it and my reading, a year or two after World War II ended, *Pan Tadeusz*, Adam Mickiewicz's great verse epic, published in 1834, about the life of provincial Lithuanian gentry, as the poet remembered it from the time of Napoleon's Russian campaign. Before World War I, Lithuania was a part of Poland, so far as Poles and the Lithuanian upper class were concerned; it had been so ever since the Lithuanian Grand Prince Jagiello was baptized in 1386, married Jadwiga, the daughter of the King of Hungary, and thus, by a dynastic sleight of hand, ascended with her to the Polish throne. The point of this historical digression is to explain why a Polish schoolboy, reading *Pan Tadeusz*, naturally did not make much of a distinction between Lithuania and Poland. In any event, this particular schoolboy being me, with my special past, made a leap that was even greater. Something in Mickiewicz's elegy, which haunted me like a forgotten melody, was nothing more or less, I realized, than my recollection of the summer and early autumn at my grandparents' property. The feat of self-aggrandizement or empathy or imagination was prodigious: what possible resemblance could there be between the modest manor house of a well-to-do Polish Jew who bought and sold agricultural produce, and the life in that fictional house, the grand domain of Mickiewicz's aristocratic and superbly old-fashioned Judge Soplica? But how much is imagination and how much is specific recollection in *Pan Tadeusz*? The poet was born in 1798. The events he described took place in 1811 and 1812, when he was a boy. In 1824 Mickiewicz was exiled by the Russians for revolutionary activities and never returned. How much could he have really remembered during the composition of a work completed more than twenty years after the fact? What were the shards from which he fashioned his gloriously detailed and textured description of the countryside and of a society that perished with its hunts, balls and quarrels? The answer is that for a poet or a novelist the distinction between what was remembered and what was imagined and made up is shadowy and unimportant. What matters is the irresistible, magnetic force exerted by a place, by a language, and, I will add, by a literature.

Mickiewicz wrote, of course, in Polish, which was his mother tongue. The gentry did not speak Lithuanian. It may be that the operation that I performed so many years ago on *Pan Tadeusz*, when I was eleven or twelve, and reconstituted when at the age of fifty-six I wrote *Wartime Lies,* exemplifies my abiding connection with the country of my birth. It is made of words, and what they evoke. Thus, in Gombrowicz's masterpiece, *Ferdydurke,* I was able to find, in the description of the school into which the adult narrator is suddenly thrust as though in a nightmare, the buried memory of the brutality of the students and certain teachers in the *gimnazjum* I attended in Cracow, and in the scene in which the narrator and his cousin discuss with relish the gentleman's sport of slapping servants, hall porters, barbers—anyone who can't hit back—my memory of being slapped on the face as a child and seeing that done to others. I did not read *Ferdydurke* until the late 1980s. In consequence, it may be even more surprising that some time ago I found a description of such blows to the face in a schoolroom—obviously in Poland, although I did not say so—in a short story I wrote as English homework, in 1948, in the high school I attended after my parents and I came to live in New York.

There should be a banner on the wall each writer faces as he sits behind his desk with the injunction AVOID CONCLUSIONS! embroidered in the appropriate language. And yet, I cannot escape asking myself about my innermost feelings. Would I have preferred remaining in Poland after the War to an emigration which, from the point of view of a very young Polish patriot—or to use a more modest formulation, a child who was brought up to love his country—could be called exile? I take into account here the fact that my initial reluctance to return to Poland as a visitor, in large part responsible for my first visit not having taken place until 1994, was related to the illegality of my parents' and my departure, and to fears (which may well have been baseless) of official chicanery, or worse, should we come back. Would I have preferred, if such a thing had been possible, to become a writer using the Polish language? As to the first question, the answer is easy. Had I remained in Poland I would not be myself today. I am not sure that I would like the person I might have become. Fortune is an ever-watchful goddess; she does not rest, and revels in striking those who seem happy. Nevertheless, I will dare to admit that I consider myself lucky to have become American, and to have the life I have had. To answer the second question involves heartbreak. I have old scores to settle with Poland. They are being liquidated by time, which has swept away most Poles who were old enough at the time of World War II to bear responsibility for what was done then or not done. As for Poles living in Poland today, I reserve judgment. The Polish language has been a source of undiluted joy for me, and it pains me to make an admission that may make me seem unfaithful to my first love. But the plain truth is that I consider myself also supremely lucky to be an American novelist, using a language of incomparable beauty and access to readers, a language that for all the difficulties I have described is totally my own. In this respect as well, my case is very different from Nabokov's, as he described it in an afterword to *Lolita*:

> My private tragedy, which cannot, and indeed should not, be anybody's concern, is that I had to abandon my natural idiom, my untrammeled, rich and infinitely docile Russian tongue for a second-rate brand of English, devoid of any of those apparatuses—the baffling mirror, the black velvet backdrop, the implied associations and traditions—which the native illusionist, frac-tails flying, can magically use to transcend the heritage in his own way.

Tragedy, surely, but one that was embedded in triumph. I know Nabokov's Russian novels only in English translation; since the translations were heavily reworked by him, it is difficult for me to distinguish the English in which they appear from the English Nabokov used in the works he wrote during his second incarnation, beginning with *The Real Life of Sebastian Knight*, which appeared in 1941. Both groups of work are masterpieces of illusionism and self-consciousness that borders on mannerism in the use of language. Were the characteristics of his Russian style different? I am incapable of providing an answer. Therefore, I follow Nabokov's advice, and take the tragedy seriously only because Nabokov's intimate wound was surely very real, as is the wound inflicted by every exile, whatever its circumstances and aftermath. The wound is one that never heals, even if one can say with Nabokov, as I do, quite heartlessly: "The break in my own destiny affords me in retrospect a syncopal kick that I would not have missed for worlds."

# The Mother Tongue
# Between Two Slices of Rye

## Gary Shteyngart

When I return to Russia, my birthplace, I cannot sleep for days. The Russian language swaddles me. The trilling *r*'s tickle the underside of my feet. Every old woman cooing to her grandson is my dead grandmother. Every glum and purposeful man picking up his wife from work in a dusty Volga sedan is my father. Every young man cursing the West with his friends over a late morning beer in the Summer Garden is me. I have fallen off the edges of the known universe, with its Palm Pilots, obnoxious vintage shops, and sleek French-Caribbean Brooklyn bistros, and have returned into a kind of elemental Shteyngart-land, a nightmare where every consonant resonates like a punch against the liver, every rare vowel makes my flanks quiver as if I'm in love.

Lying in bed in my hotel room I am hurt to the quick by the words from an idiotic pop song: "Please don't bother me," a cheerful young girl is singing on a Russian music channel, "I'm going back to my mama's house."

If I'm in some cheap Soviet hell-hole of a hotel, I can hear the housekeepers screaming at each other. "Lera, bitch, give me back my twenty."

"You, Vera, are the bitch," says her colleague. These words *Ti, Vera, suka* replay themselves as an endless mantra as I sink my face into a skimpy, dandruff-smelling pillow from Brezhnev times. For the time being, Lera and Vera are my relatives, my loved ones, my everything. I want to walk out of my room and say, in my native tongue, "Lera, Vera, here is twenty rubles for each of you. Ladies, dear ones, let's have some tea and cognac in the bar downstairs."

If I'm in a Western hotel, one of Moscow's Marriotts, say, I try to tune into the airplane-like hum of the central AC and banish Russian from my mind. I am surrounded by burnished mahogany, heated towel racks, and all sorts of business class accoutrements ("Dear Guest," little cards address me in English, "your overall satisfaction is our ultimate goal"), but when I open the window I face a stark Soviet-era building, where the Veras and Leras carry on at full pitch, grandmas coo to children, young men while away the morning hours in the courtyard with beer and invective.

In order to fall asleep, I try speaking to myself in English. "Hi there! Was' up? What are you doing Thursday? I have to see my analyst from 4:00 to 4:45. I can be downtown by 5:30. When do you get off work?" I repeat the last words to my phantom New York friend over and over, trying to regain my American balance, the sense that rationalism, psychiatry and a few sour apple martinis can take care of the past, because, as the Marriott people say, overall satisfaction is our ultimate goal. "When do you get off work? When do you get off work? When do you get off work? Hi there!" But it's no use.

*Please don't bother me, I'm going back to my mama's house.*
*Lera, you bitch, give me my twenty rubles.*

And in a final insult, an old Soviet anthem from my youth, hummed through the back channels of memory, the little chutes and trap doors that connect the right brain and the left ventricle through which pieces of primordial identity keep falling out.

> *The seagull is flapping its wings*
> *Calling us to our duty*
> *Pioneers and friends and all our comrades*
> *Let us set out for the journey ahead*

Sliced down the middle, splayed like a red snapper in a Chinatown restaurant, stuffed with *kh* and *sh* sounds instead of garlic and ginger, I lie in a Moscow or St. Petersburg hotel bed, tearful and jet-lagged, whispering to the ceiling in a brisk, staccato tone, maniacally naming all the things for which the Russian language is useful—ordering mushroom and barley soup, directing the cab driver to some forgotten grave, planning the putsch that will for once install an enlightened government. *Khh . . . Shh . . . Rrrrr.*

Home at last.

*Veliky moguchi russki yazik.* The Great and Mighty Russian Tongue is how my first language bills itself. Throughout its seventy-year tenure, bureaucratic Soviet-speak had inadvertently stripped it of much of its greatness and might (try casually saying the acronym OSOAVIAKHIM, which denotes the Association for Assistance of Defense, Aircraft and Chemical Development). But in 1977 the beleaguered Russian tongue can still put on quite a show for a five-year-old boy in a Leningrad metro station. The trick is to use giant copper block letters nailed to a granite wall, signifying both pomp and posterity, an upper-case paean to an increasingly lower-case Soviet state. The words, gracing the walls of the Technological Institute station, read as follows:

1959—SOVIET SPACE ROCKET
REACHES THE SURFACE OF THE MOON

Take that, Neil Armstrong.

1934—SOVIET SCIENTISTS CREATE
THE FIRST CHAIN REACTION THEORY

So that's where it all began.

1974—THE BUILDING OF THE BAIKAL-AMUR
MAIN RAILROAD TRUNK HAS BEEN INITIATED

Now what the hell does that mean? Ah, but Baikal-Amur sounds so beautiful—Baikal the famous (and now famously polluted) Siberian lake, a centerpiece of Russian myth; Amur (amour?) could almost be another word Russian has gleefully appropriated from the French (it is, in fact, the name of a region in the Russian Far East).

I'm five years old, felt boots tight around my feet and ankles, what might be half of a bear or several Soviet beavers draped around my shoulders, my mouth open so wide that, as my father keeps warning me, "a crow will fly in there." I am in awe. The metro, with its wall-length murals of the broad-chested revolutionary working class that never was, with its hectares of granite and marble vestibules, is a mouth-opener to be sure. And the words! Those words whose power seems not only persuasive, but, to this five-year-old kid already obsessed with science fiction, extra-terrestrial. The wise aliens have landed and WE ARE THEM. And this is the language we use. The great and mighty Russian tongue.

Meanwhile, a metro train full of sweaty comrades pulls into the station, ready to take us north to the Hermitage or the Dostoyevsky museum. But what use is there for the glum truth of Rembrandt's returning prodigal son or a display of the great novelist's piss pots, when the future of the human race, denuded of its mystery, is right here for all to see. SOVIET SCIENTISTS CREATE THE FIRST CHAIN REACTION THEORY. Forget the shabby polyester-clad human element around you, the unique Soviet metro smell of a million barely washed proletarians being sucked through an enormous marble tube. There it is, kid, in copper capital letters. What more do you want?

Some two years later, in Queens, New York, I am being inducted into a different kind of truth. I am standing amidst a gaggle of boys in white shirts and skullcaps, and girls in long dresses wailing a prayer in an ancient language. Adults are on hand to make sure we are all singing in unison; that is to say, refusing to wail is not an option. *"Sh'ima Yisrael,"* I wail, obediently, *"Adonai Eloheinu, Adonai echad."*

Hear, O Israel, the Lord is our God, the Lord is One.

I'm not sure what the Hebrew words mean (there is an English translation in the prayer book, only I don't know any English either), but I know the tone. There is something plaintive in the way we boys and girls are beseeching the Almighty. What we're doing, I think, is supplicating. And the members of my family are no strangers to supplication. We are Soviet Jewish refugees in America ("refu-Jews," the joke would go). We are poor. We are at the mercy of others: Food Stamps from the American government, financial aid from refugee organizations, second-hand Batman and Green Lantern t-shirts and scuffed furniture gathered by kind American Jews. I am sitting in the cafeteria of the Hebrew school, surrounded first by the walls of this frightening institution—a gray piece of modern architecture liberally inlaid with panes of tinted glass—with its large, sweaty rabbi, its young, underpaid teachers, and its noisy, undisciplined American Jewish kids, and, in a larger sense, surrounded by America: a complex, media-driven, gadget-happy society, whose images and language are the lingua franca of the world and whose flowery odors and easy smiles are completely beyond me. I'm sitting there, alone at a lunch table, a small boy in over-sized glasses and a tight checkered Russian shirt, perhaps the product of some Checkered Shirt Factory #12 in Sverdlovsk, and what I'm doing is, I'm talking to myself.

I'm talking to myself in Russian.

Am I saying "1959—SOVIET SPACE ROCKET REACHES THE SURFACE OF THE MOON"? It's very possible. Am I recounting the contents of the Vorontsovski Palace in Yalta, where, just a year ago, I proved myself smarter than the rest of the tour group (and won my mother's undying love) by pointing out that the palace resembled the contours of a neighboring mountain? It could be. Am I nervously whispering an old Russian childhood ditty (one that would later find its way into one of my stories written as an adult): "Let it always be sunny, let there always be Mommy, let there always be blue skies, let there always be me"? Very possible. Because what I need now, in this unhappy, alien place, is Mommy, the woman who sews my mittens to my great overcoat, for otherwise I will lose them, as I have already lost the bottle of glue, lined notebook and crayons that accompany me to first grade.

One thing is certain—along with Mommy, and Papa, and one sweet kid, the son of liberal American parents who have induced him to play with me—the Russian language is my friend. It's comfortable around me. It knows things the noisy brats around me, who laugh and point as I intone my Slavic sibilants, will never understand. The way the Vorontsovski Palace resembles the mountain next to it. The way you get frisked at the Leningrad Airport, the customs guard taking off your hat and feeling it up for contraband diamonds. The way SOVIET SCIENTISTS CREATE[D] THE FIRST CHAIN REACTION THEORY in 1934. All this the great and mighty Russian language knows. All this it whispers to me at night, as I lie haunted by childhood insomnia.

Teachers try to intervene. They tell me to get rid of some of my Russian furs. Trim my bushy hair a little. Stop talking to myself in Russian. Be more, you know, *normal.* I am invited to play with the liberals' son, a gentle, well-fed fellow who seems lost in the wilderness of Eastern Queens. We go to a pizza parlor, and, as I inhale a slice, a large string of gooey Parmesan cheese gets stuck in my throat. Using most of my fingers, I try to pull the cheese out. I choke. I gesture about. I panic. I moo at our chaperone, a graceful American mama. *Pomogite!* I mouth. Help! I am caught in a world of cheap endless cheese. I can see a new placard for the Leningrad metro. 1979—FIRST SOVIET CHILD CHOKES ON CAPITALIST PIZZA. When it's all over, I sit there shuddering, my hands covered with spittle and spent Parmesan. This is no way to live.

And then one day I fall in love with cereal. We are too poor to afford toys at this point, but we do have to eat. Cereal is food. It tastes grainy, easy and light, with a hint of false fruitiness. It tastes the way America feels. I'm obsessed with the fact that many cereal boxes come with prizes inside, which seems to me an unprecedented miracle. Something for nothing. My favorite comes in a box of a cereal called Honey Combs, a box featuring a healthy white kid—as a sufferer of asthma, I begin to accept him as an important role-model—on a bike flying through the sky (many years later I learn he's probably "popping a wheelie"). What you get inside each box of Honey Combs are small license plates to be tied to the rear of your bicycle. The license plates are much smaller than the real thing but they have a nice metallic heft to them. I keep getting MICHIGAN, a very simple plate, white letters on a black base. I trace the word with my finger. I speak it aloud, getting most of the sounds wrong. MEESHUGAN.

When I have a thick stack of plates, I hold them in my hand and spread them out like playing cards. I casually throw them on my dingy mattress, then scoop them up and press them to my chest for no reason. I hide them under my pillow, then ferret them out like a demented post-Soviet dog. Each plate is terribly unique. Some states present themselves as "America's Dairyland," others wish to "Live Free or Die." What I need now, in a very serious way, is to get an actual bike.

In America the distance between wanting something and having it delivered to your living room is not terribly great. I want a bike, so some rich American (they're all rich) gives me a bike. A rusted red monstrosity with the spokes coming dangerously undone, but what do you want? I tie the license plate to the bicycle, and I spend most of my day wondering which plate to use, citrus-sunny FLORIDA or snowy VERMONT. This is what America is about: choice.

I don't have much choice in pals, but there's a one-eyed girl in our building complex whom I have sort of befriended. She's tiny and scrappy, and poor just like us. We're suspicious of each other at first, but I'm an immigrant and she has one eye, so we're even. The girl rides around on a half-broken bike just like mine, and she keeps falling and scraping herself (rumor is that's how she lost her eye) and bawling whenever her palms get bloodied, her head raised up to the sky. One day she sees me riding my banged-up bicycle with the Honey Combs license plate clanging behind me and she screams "MICHIGAN! MICHIGAN!" And I ride ahead, smiling and tooting my bike horn, proud of the English letters that are attached somewhere below my ass. Michigan! Michigan! with its bluish-black license plate the color of my friend's remaining eye. Michigan, with its delicious American name. How lucky one must be to live there.

Vladimir Girshkin, the struggling young immigrant hero of my first novel, *The Russian Debutante's Handbook,* shares a few characteristics with me, notably his penchant for counting money in Russian, which, according to the book, is "the language of longing, of homeland and Mother, his money-counting language." And also, I might add, the language of *fear.* When the ATM coughs out a bushel of cash or I am trying to perform a magic trick with my checkbook, trying to glean something from nothing, I leave English behind. American dollars, the lack of which constitutes an immigrant's most elemental fright, are denominated entirely in the Russian language. And so with shaking hands, the fictional Vladimir Girshkin and the all-too-real Gary Shteyngart count a short stack of greenbacks, a record of our worth and accomplishment in our adopted land: *"Vosem-desyat dollarov . . . Sto dollarov . . . Sto-dvadtsat' dollarov . . ."*

Many of my dreams are also dreamt in Russian, especially those infused with terror. There's one, for instance, where I emerge into a sepia-toned Manhattan, its skyscrapers covered by the chitinous shells of massive insects with water-bug antennae waving menacingly from their roofs. "What has happened?" I ask an unmistakably American passer-by, a pretty young woman in a middle-class pullover.

*"Nichevo,"* she answers in Russian ("it's nothing"), with a bored Slavic shrug of the shoulders, just as I notice a pair of insect-like mandibles protruding from the base of her jaw. And I wake up whispering *bozhe moi, bozhe moi.* My God, my God.

And when terror informs my waking world, when an airplane's engines for some reason quit their humming mid-flight, when a big man with murder in his nostrils turns the corner and walks right into me, I think *Za shto?* What for? Why me? Why now? Why am I to die like this? Is it fair? It's a question addressed not to the Heavens, which I'm guessing are fairly empty of God, but to the Russian language itself, the repository of my sense of unfairness, a language in which awful things happen inexplicably and irrevocably.

After we come to the States, many of my more adaptable fellow immigrants quickly part ways with their birth languages and begin singing Michael Jackson's "Billie Jean" with remarkable accuracy and hip-swinging panache. The reason I still speak, think, dream, quake in fear, and count money in Russian has to do with a series of decisions my parents make when we're still greenhorns. They insist that only Russian be spoken in the home. It's a trade-off. While I will retain my Russian, my parents will struggle with the new language, nothing being more instructive than having a child prattle on in English at the dinner table.

Our house is Russian down to the last buckwheat kernel of kasha. When English does make its appearance, it is scribbled on a series of used IBM punch cards from my father's computer classes. I handle the punch cards with the same awe as I do the Honey Combs license plates, intrigued as much by their crisp, beige, American feel as by the words and phrases my father has written upon them, English on one side, Russian on the other. I remember, for some reason, the following words—"industry (*promishlenost*), "teapot" (*chainik*), "heart attack" (*infarkt*), "symbolism" (*symvolizm*), "mortgage" (*zaklad*), and "ranch" (*rancho*).

The second decision is mostly economic. We cannot afford a television, so instead of the Dukes of Hazzard, I turn to the collected works of Anton Chekhov, eight battered volumes of which still sit on my bookshelves. And when we find a little black-and-white Zenith in the trash can outside our building, I am only allowed to watch it for half an hour a week, not enough time to understand why Buck Rogers is trapped in the 25th century or why the Incredible Hulk is sometimes green and sometimes not. Without television there is absolutely nothing to talk about with any of the children at school. It turns out these loud little porkers have very little interest in "Gooseberries" or "Lady with Lapdog," and it is impossible in the early 1980s to hear a sentence spoken by a child without an allusion to something shown on TV.

So I find myself doubly handicapped, living in a world where I speak neither the actual language, English, nor the second and almost just as important language—television. For most of my American childhood I have the wretched sensation that fin-de-siècle Yalta with its idle, beautiful women and conflicted, lecherous men lies somewhere between the Toys "R" Us superstore and the multiplex.

Around this time, I start writing in English with gusto. I write for the same reasons other curious children write: loneliness, boredom, the transgressive excitement of building your own world out of letters, a world not sanctioned by family and school. The latter becomes my target. While I patiently wail my *"Sh'ma Yisrael,"* praying that God will indeed take mercy on me, that he will make the young Hebrew School Judeans stop teasing me for my cardboard sweater and my anxious, sweaty brow, for being a bankrupt Russian in a silver-tinseled American world, I also decide to act.

I write my own Torah. It's called the Gnorah, an allusion to my nickname Gary Gnu, the name of an obscure television antelope which I have never seen. The Gnorah is a very libertine version of the Old Testament, with lots of musical numbers, singing prophets, and horny eleven-year-old takes on biblical themes. Exodus becomes Sexodus, for instance. Henry Miller would have been proud.

The Gnorah is written on an actual scroll, which I somehow manage to type up sideways so that it looks like an actual Torah. I hit the IBM Selectric keyboard with a giddy, nerdish excitement. Thousands of sacrilegious English words pour out in a matter of days, words that aren't inflected with my still-heavy Russian accent. Impatiently, I blow on passages deleted with white-out, knowing somehow that my life is about to change. And it does. The Gnorah receives wide critical acclaim from the students of the Solomon Schechter Hebrew Day School of Queens—a relief from the rote memorization of the Talmud, from the aggressive shouting of blessings and counter-blessings before and after lunch, from the ornery rabbi who claims the Jews brought on the Holocaust by their over-consumption of delicious pork products. The Gnorah gets passed around and quoted. It doesn't quite make me acceptable or beloved. Only owning a twenty-seven-inch Sony Trinitron and a wardrobe from Stern's department store can do that. But it helps me cross the line from unclubbable fruitcake to tolerated eccentric. Tell me, is there anything writing can't do?

The Gnorah marks the end of Russian as my primary tongue and the beginning of my true assimilation into American English. I want to be loved so badly, it verges on mild insanity. I devote most of my school hours, time that should be spent analyzing Talmudic interpretations of how a cow becomes a steak, writing stories for my classmates, stories that poke fun at our measly lives, stories filled with references to television shows I barely know, stories shorn of any allusion to the Russia I've left behind or to the pages of Chekhov patiently yellowing on my book-shelves. A progressive young teacher sets aside time at the end of the English class for me to read these stories, and, as I read, my classmates yelp and giggle appreciatively, a great victory for the written word in this part of Queens.

But soon my pre-adolescent writing career is cut short. My

family is not so poor anymore and can afford to shell out one thousand dollars for a salmon-colored twenty-seven-inch Sony Trinitron. The delivery of this Sony Trinitron is possibly the happiest moment of my life. Finally, in a real sense, I become a naturalized citizen of this country. I turn it on, and I never turn it off. For the next ten years, I will write almost nothing.

I have begun this essay with a sleepless trip to contemporary Russia, a trip bathed in the anxious sounds of the mother tongue, and I have come to the end with a child's farewell to the language that once choreographed his entire world. But memory, which in the Russian sense is often just a flimsy cover for nostalgia, begs for a different ending.

So I will conclude elsewhere, at a place called the Ann Mason Bungalow Colony in the Catskill Mountains. Even the poorest Russian cannot live without a summer *dacha,* and so every June we, along with other Russian families, rent one of a dozen of little barrack-style bungalows (white plaster exterior with a hint of cheap wood around the windows) not far from the old Jewish Borscht Belt hotels. My mother and I sneak into the nearby Tamarack Lodge, where Eddie Fisher and Buddy Hackett once shared a stage, to witness giant, tanned American Jews lying belly-up next to an Olympic-size outdoor pool or sleep walking to the auditorium in bedroom slippers to watch Neil Diamond in *The Jazz Singer.* This is probably the grandest sight I have come across in the ten or eleven years of my existence. I immediately vow to work hard so that one day I can afford this kind of lifestyle and pass it on to my children (the Tamarack Lodge has since closed; I have no children).

Back at the Ann Mason Bungalow Colony, we survive without

daily screenings of *The Jazz Singer* and the pool can fit maybe a half-dozen small Russian children at a time. Ann Mason, the proprietor, is an old Yiddish-spouting behemoth with three muu-muus to her wardrobe. Her summer population during weekdays consists almost entirely of Soviet children and the grandmothers entrusted with them—the parents are back in New York work-ing to keep us all in buckwheat. The children (there are about ten of us from Leningrad, Kiev, Kishinev and Vilnius) adore Ann Mason's husband, a ridiculous, pot-bellied, red-bearded runt named Marvin, an avid reader of the Sunday funny papers whose fly is always open and whose favorite phrase is "Everybody in the pool!" When Ann Mason cuts enough coupons, she and Marvin take some of us to the Ponderosa Steakhouse for T-bones and mashed potatoes. The all-you-can-eat salad bar is the nexus of capitalism and gluttony we've all been waiting for.

Ann Mason's Bungalow Colony sits on the slope of a hill, beneath which lies a small but very prodigious brook, from which my father and I extract enormous catfish and an even larger fish whose English name I have never learned (in Russian it's called a *sig;* the Oxford-Russian dictionary tells me, rather obliquely, that it is a "freshwater fish of the salmon family"). On the other side of the brook there is a circular hay field which belongs to a rabidly anti-Semitic Polish man who will hunt us down with his German shepherd if we go near, or so our grand-mothers tell us.

Our summers are spent being chased by these grandmothers, each intent on feeding us fruits and farmer's cheese, which, along with kasha in the morning, form the cornerstones of our mad diets. Shouts of *"frukti!"* (fruits) and *"tvorog!"* (farmer's cheese) echo above the anti-Semite's mysterious hay field. By sundown a new word is added to the grandmothers' vocabulary, *"sviter!"*—a desperate appeal for us to put on sweaters against the mountain cold.

These children are as close as I have come to compatriots. I look forward to being with them all year. There is no doubt that several of the girls are maturing into incomparable beauties, their tiny faces acquiring a round Eurasian cast, slim-hipped tomboyish bodies growing soft here and there. But what I love most are the sounds of our hoarse, excited voices. The Russian nouns lacing the barrage of English verbs, or vice versa (*"babushka, oni poshli* shopping *vmeste v ellenvilli"*—"grandma, they went shopping together in Ellenville").

Fresh from my success with the Gnorah, I decide to write the lyrics for a music album, popular American songs with a Russian inflection. Madonna's "Like a Virgin" becomes "Like a Sturgeon." There are paeans to babushkas, to farmer's cheese, to budding sexuality rendered with a trilled *r* that sounds sexier than we think. We record these songs on a tape recorder I buy at a drugstore. For the album cover photograph I pose as Bruce Springsteen on his *Born in the USA* album, dressed in jeans and a t-shirt, a red baseball cap sticking out of my back pocket. Several of the girls pose around my "Bruce." They are dressed in their finest skirts and blouses, along with hopeful application of mascara and lipstick. "Born in the USSR" is what we call the album. (*"I was bo-ho-rn down in-uh Le-nin-grad . . . wore a big fur* shapka *on my head, yeah . . . "*)

We await the weekends when our parents will come, exhausted from their American jobs, the men eager to take off their shirts and point their hairy chests at the sky, the women to talk in low tones about their husbands. We cram into a tiny stationwagon and head for one of the nearest towns where, along with a growing Hasidic population, there is a theater that shows last summer's movies for two dollars (giant bag of popcorn with fake butter—fifty cents). On the return trip to the Ann Mason Bungalow Colony, sitting on each other's laps, we discuss the finer points of *E.T. the Extra-Terrestrial*. I wonder aloud why the film never ventured into outer space, never revealed to us the wrinkled fellow's planet, his birthplace and true home.

We continue our Russo-American discussion into the night, the stars lighting up the bull's-eye of the anti-Semitic hay field, our grandmothers mumbling the next day's rations of kasha and sweaters in their sleep. Tomorrow, a long stretch of non-competitive badminton. The day after that, Marvin will bring out the funny papers and we will laugh at Beetle Bailey and Garfield, not always knowing why we're laughing. It's something like happiness, the not knowing why.

# Boswell and Mrs. Miller

## James Campbell

When James Boswell took the low road from Scotland to London in 1762, to seek his fortune and eventually to write the *Life of Johnson,* he required no passport to cross the border; but as he went, he imagined his whole being receiving the stamp of improvement. Boswell's overwhelming purpose in life was to better himself; in order to do so, he was ready to slough off the rough Scots "Jamie," and admit the politer, anglicized James. In London, however, Boswell encountered an unexpected and unwanted reminder of home on the southern air. "Mrs. Miller's Glasgow tongue excruciated me," he wrote in his journal for March 17, 1763. "I resolved never again to dine where a Scotchwoman from the West was allowed to feed with us."

The Scotchwoman from the West must have made an awful din. Boswell suggests a genteel table upset by a barking ruffian. We notice that, while he "dines," Mrs. Miller "feeds." It comes as a surprise to learn that Mrs. Miller was the wife of Thomas Miller, Lord Advocate of Scotland, the country's highest ranking legal figure. She would have been considered, and would have thought herself, a member of the gentry. Boswell's annoyance and embarrassment tell us that it was common for respectable society figures in mid-eighteenth-century Scotland to speak a form of what is called Older Scots, a generic designation for the dialect tongue that wags across time, from the middle ages to the present day. Boswell himself could only have avoided sounding like Mrs. Miller by making a positive effort not to.

How, exactly, does Mrs. Miller speak? She says "aff" for off and "oot" for out; "ben the hoose" to mean indoors, and "gree-tan" for weeping. Mrs. Miller gets wired intae her dener, while Boswell and the others are carefully keeping their elbows off the table. She uses idioms and peculiar grammatical constructions which he has been taking pains to expunge for years: "Ah doot Jamie canny tell a rich wumman bi a puir," she thinks, sensing Boswell's snobbish contempt. "He haes a face on him aye that wad soor milk." Catching his angry eye, she cries out, "Dinna fash yersel'," before turning back to her "parridge," the common name she gives to the tastiest of dishes. To Boswell and the assembled company, Mrs. Miller seems incapable of grasping the difference between "those" and "they" (or thae), and equally incapable of pronouncing the flat "a," so that references to those apples in the dish over there inevitably tumble out of her mouth as "thae aipples," no matter how she tries to prevent it happening. She speaks of the dish as "thon ashet yonder." She havers on about her "faither" and "mirra" and the "wee wean," her child, and "hoo i wiz glaiket but bonny forby." When she does use the flat "a," it's in the wrong place: water, for example, drips off Mrs. Miller's tongue as "waa'er." Imagine these deviations spread across the entire field of English speech, and you have some idea of the sound that "excruciated" Boswell.

Mrs. Miller cannot be allowed back to the table; if she should be, Boswell will refuse to join in. A few weeks earlier, he had reflected that it would be wiser in future—more socially advantageous, in other words—to avoid contact altogether with the compatriots who arrived in London and came knocking on his door. Particularly those who embarrassed him by speaking in "the abominable Glasgow tongue."

I know Mrs. Miller well. I can hear her clearly. With a few shifts in flats and sharps, a slight increase or reduction in the incidence of glottal stops (try removing any hint of a "t" from "waa'er" and replacing it with an emphasis on the second syllable), her descendants in Glasgow speak today as she did two and a half centuries ago. Mrs. Miller's speech reflected the natural West of Scotland way of talking; it was Boswell, powdering his palate from a compact of airs and affectations, who was trying to groom himself to "talk suddron" (southern). It was fashionable among some, though not all, Scottish ladies and gentlemen of the day to do so. Boswell came from a well-to-do family of land-owning lawyers from the rural Southwest, and attended Glasgow University. He had taken lessons in elocution in Edinburgh from Thomas Sheridan, father of the playwright Richard Brinsley, and he would have been familiar with the little books of "Scotticisms," published in the 1750s and 60s, containing alphabetical lists of words and phrases that Scots in public life were advised to avoid, especially when indulging in commercial or social intercourse with their English or foreign counterparts. Mrs. Miller's offence, on being "allowed to feed" at a polite table in London, was to disregard the presumed linguistic etiquette.

Boswell's objections make him sound like a boor and even a traitor. But he was less of a snob than he might seem. His attachment to the great natural democrat Dr. Johnson was genuine and philosophically grounded, and his feeling for Scotland was deep. Eventually, he married a Scotchwoman from the West, and lived with her in Edinburgh, in the East. However, his severe attitude to the Glasgow tongue is just as familiar to someone who was born and brought up in the city—as I was—as the tongue itself. The two ways of speaking may be separated into "Glasgow" and "Glesca," after the different pronunciations of the city's name. The tongue has divided families, neighbors and neighborhoods; it has drawn a notional segregation marker through the city. A refined Glasgow speaker might go out of his way to avoid contact with a Glesca speaker. Each would recognize the social standing of the other as soon as they opened their mouths. Mr. Glasgow might treat Mr. Glesca and his "patter" as a topic of couthie humour, a kind of Caledonian minstrelsy, which is calculated to amuse; similarly, the Glesca man can only bring himself to pronounce the official name of his city, "Glasgow," in a pointed, comical way. To attempt it in ordinary conversation would be to invite ridicule from his friends. The Glasgow man probably believes (without having given it much thought) that the other who says "Glesca" does so out of an inability to pronounce "Glasgow." It is possible that neither is aware that the "lower" pronunciation reflects the medieval spelling of the city's name; in the fourteenth and fifteenth centuries, Glasgow was "Glescu," and must have been pronounced that way by the Boswells and Mrs. Millers alike.

The linguistic division, which developed fully round about 1600 with the Union of the Crowns of England and Scotland, has also split individuals. There is no better illustration of the double-sidedness of the Scottish tongue than the national poet himself. For both his daily life and his poetry, Robert Burns had two dialects: Older Scots and Standard English. Sometimes he employed them both in a single sentence, or poetic couplet, as in the well-known lines,

*The best-laid schemes o' mice an' men*
*Gang aft a-gley.*

"To a Mouse," like many Burns poems, is written in a combination of Scots and English, but the dominant flavor is Scots, even when dialect vocabulary is used scarcely—"Wee, sleekit, cow'rin, tim'rous beastie." The same was true of Burns's everyday speech. To the neighboring farmers in Ayrshire (Boswell's county, as it happens, some fifty miles to the south-west of Glasgow), Burns spoke like this:

> I'm sitten down here, after seven and forty miles ridin, e'en as forjesket and forniaw'd as forfoughten cock, to gie you some notion o' my landlowper-like stravaguin sin the sorrowfu' hour that I sheuk hands and parted wi' auld Reekie. . . .
>
> I hae daunder'd owre a' the kintra frae Dumbar to Selcraig, and hae forgather'd wi' monie a guid fallow and monie a weelfar'd hizzie—I met wi' twa dink quines in particular, ane o' them a sonsie, fine fodgel lass, baith braw and bonnie.

Yet he was capable of adopting a cultivated manner when circumstances required it. For the men and women with whom he socialized in the drawing-rooms of Edinburgh ("auld Reekie"), on whom he sometimes was forced to depend financially, he adopted a different voice altogether:

> I cannot bear the idea of leaving Edinburgh without seeing you—I know not how to account for it—I am strangely taken with some people; nor am I often mistaken. You are a stranger to me; but I am an odd being: some yet unnamed feelings; things not principles, but better than whims, carry me farther than boasted reason ever did a Philosopher.

The letter in Scots, dealing with one of Burns's favorite subjects (the "twa dink quines" might elsewhere be described as two comely wenches), is to the poet's friend William Nicol, a schoolmaster; the other, written in the same year, 1787, is to Agnes McLehose, a more genteel-sounding Scotchwoman from the West than Mrs. Miller, with whom Burns conducted a brief courtship.

Scots has numerous regional variations, of which Burns's Ayrshire and Mrs. Miller's Glesca are only two. All are related, and all forms of Scots are likewise linked to standard English. The use of Scots for day-to-day purposes was still common in the time of Burns and Boswell. Two hundred and fifty years before that, it was universal. For the past century and a half, however, Scots has been declared dead, or regarded as petering out (or else it is in the throes of a revival). Robert Louis Stevenson, born into a middle-class Edinburgh family in 1850, picked up a fair sprinkling of Scots from servants and gardeners, which he put to spirited use in poems and letters, and occasionally in short stories such as "Thrawn Janet"; but he was aware as he did so that he was indulging a linguistic form of nostalgia. Stevenson recalled his grandfather, born a year or two after Burns's effusions, as "one of the last, I suppose, to speak broad Scots and be a gentleman." The country folk of present-day Ayrshire, tuning into *EastEnders* and *Friends*, and conversing via the transatlantic line with their emigrant cousins in North America, no longer talk to one another as Burns did to Willie Nicol, nor do they use much of the vocabulary that gives poems such as "To a Mouse" and "Tam o' Shanter" their distinct fibre. There is, in a sense, less space for the dialect; the distances that separate groups of people have shrunk, and we are apt to address our neighbors in a language we trust they will understand.

Yet Scots is still alive. It is current in ways that may be barely noticed. Boys and girls in the streets of Glasgow today, for example, would find the idiom of this sixteenth-century ballad quite familiar; should you be passing by, you might hear them speak in a way that is close to it:

*As I was a-walkin all alane*
*I spied twa corbies makkin a mane.*
*The tane untae the ither did say-o:*
*Whaur sall we gang tae dine the day-o.*

*In ahent yon auld fell dyke,*
*I wot there lies a new slain knight.*
*And naebody kens that he lies there-o*
*But his hawk an' his hound an' his lady fair-o.*

"Doubles" or "doubling" are often evoked in discussions of Scottish literature, with reference made to Stevenson's *Strange Case of Dr. Jekyll and Mr. Hyde* and James Hogg's *Confessions of a Justified Sinner,* and even to poems like "Tam o' Shanter," which inhabit a split-level reality—this world, and the world of ghaisties, witches and warlocks into which Tam stumbles. Indeed, "doubling" is an actual feature of the language in which a large portion of Scottish literature is composed. There is a formulation, originally made by the poet Edwin Muir but so often cited as to have become a commonplace, that modern Scottish writers who make use of the dialect feel in one language (Scots) while they think in another (English).

The conflict between the two elements continues to occur in Scotland today. It was played out in my family living room on the southside of Glasgow in the late 1950s and early 60s. We were a typical working-class family with typical aspirations to be more middle-class. I was carefully brought up to speak properly (or, as the people who don't speak properly say, "speak polite"). But in my mid-teens, as part of a private revolution, I began a linguistic migration back to the Older Scots. I didn't know then that that was the name of the dialect which I heard all around me ("As I was a-walkin all alane"); there must have been something in the rougher way of talking that suited my adolescent storm. My parents took the position, let's say, of Boswell, whereas I found myself cast as Mrs. Miller. The process coincided with my falling in with a new crowd of friends, who came from a poorer, indeed notorious, area of Glasgow, the Gorbals. There was nothing in my friends' behavior to deserve the stamp of notoriety, but geography is itself the marker of repute in most big cities, and Glasgow is no exception. Each evening, to the alarm of those who cared for my welfare and my future, I walked past the neatly trimmed hedges of our street and strolled into the world of tenement closes, pens, yards, and dunnies. And, like Boswell but in reverse, I exchanged my tongue on the way. Leaving my jacket at home and pittan oan ma jaiket; leaving Glasgow and daun'erin owre tae Glesca.

It is hardly unusual for teenagers to have one language for the playground and another for the classroom or, as in this case, one for the street and another for the living room. Here the scene was dramatized into a choice between dark and light, like the choice Tam o' Shanter faced as he rode home on his grey mare Meg after an evening sat "bousin at the nappy." My mother, like most of the mothers round about, had barely heard of Boswell; but she knew all about "the abominable Glasgow tongue." By gentling their vowels, and those of their children, my parents were doing what generations of lowly folk had done before: they were trying to "get on," or, in Boswellian terms, to make themselves welcome to feed at the table. The streets of Glasgow were crowded with people who had not got on. They were poor, they were out of work, they drank too much and had troublesome dealings with the law, and frequently with everyone else who came near them. It seemed they could not even negotiate the vowels and consonants of the language, the Queen's English, with proper competence. *Who'll give you a job when you speak like that?* It was held up before us as a character failure.

There were respectable people who said "grun" when they meant ground, who couldn't shape the "ou" in house, or the "ea" in dead and bread, but said "hoose" and "deid" and "breid"; who said "hame" for home; who had difficulty in completing simple words, such as of, all, Dad (o', a', Da'), and could not master the pronunciation of blind, but had to settle for "blinn" instead. But mostly they lived in the country, like my mother's adored Uncle Willie, a shepherd on a Highland farm, where a Scots tongue was regarded as a "hertsome" thing. In the country, the broad Scots accent sounded healthier, just as the milk and the eggs that came straight from the farm on to our breakfast table tasted better.

If these acceptable Scots speakers were not country folk, they were elderly, rooted in old ways and the nineteenth century, like Grandma and Grandpa. For it is an oddity of the linguistic politics I am discussing that when my sisters and I went to visit our grandparents, born within the lifetime of Robert Louis Stevenson, we were greeted by the auld tongue. "C'wa ben the hoose," our grandmother would say on our arrival. A light fall of rain she'd call a "smirr," or a "smirrie rain"; wet children were "fair drookit." If she should "jalouse," or suspect, a cold, she gave us loathesome brandy. Like many of her class and generation, her speech, though principally English, dawdled naturally and frequently amid the Older Scots. She said "gang" for going, "havers" for nonsense, called boys and girls "chiels and quines," called a drain a "stank." If it was "dreich" outside, it was "a scunner" to her. Many of the words from Burns's vocabulary would have come naturally, and still do to large numbers of Scottish people: "bide" for live, for example; "thole," to endure. Grandma would never have heard of Hugh MacDiarmid, the greatest twentieth-century practitioner of Scots, but she would have understood his verse:

> *Mars is braw in crammasy,*
> *Venus in a green silk goun,*
> *The auld mune shak's her gowden feathers,*
> *Their starry talk's a wheen o' blethers,*
> *Nane for thee a thochtie sparin',*
> *Earth, thou bonnie broukit bairn!*

Meanwhile, my elder sisters were being sent to an elocution teacher to comb out as many tholes, bides, dreichs, and drookits from their speech as possible. They pranced around the house saying, "How—now—brown—cow," in theatrical fashion. Boswell, recalling his own youthful instruction from Thomas Sheridan, would have smiled on them.

My mother and Boswell had a formidable range of good intentions in their armory. These included education, respectability, worldly acceptance. On our side, Mrs. Miller and I (though I did not yet realize it) had literature. Only much later did I

understand that the language spoken by my friends in the Gorbals, by Grandma and Grandpa and Uncle Willie with his shepherd's crook, and by the chiels and quines in Ayrshire and
throughout Scotland, was not corrupt at all. Each regional varia-
tion, including the Glesca dialect, was derived from the Older
Scots, the language used by the great fifteenth-century "makaris,"
William Dunbar and Robert Henryson. The boys and girls in the
neighboring streets, who said "thae aipples," did not do so out of
an inability to pronounce "these apples," or because they found
it an embarrassment to "speak polite," as when prodded by
teachers to say "Glasgow" instead of "Glesca"; they were simply,
unwittingly, carrying on the Older Scots idiom which centuries
of elocutional refinement had failed to smooth out. "Doon,"
"gaun," "grun," "dinnae" and a thousand other features of present-
day Glasgow speech are retentions from a way of talking that was
once common to all the people of Lowland Scotland (as "gotten"
and "the fall," no longer used in English English, are retained in
the American). "Thae aipples yonder, lyan oan the brae ahent
the dyke, are sweit and bonie" is a sentence which my Gorbals
comrades and the poet William Dunbar (1460–1513) would understand, as one. "These apples on the hill, over there behind
the wall, are sweet and delicious" is not.

Do I "feel" in Scots, despite thinking in English? On occasion,
yes, especially to accommodate certain rushes of skepticism or
joy that I take to be native. Or to express anger, or engage with
children and animals. Scots words are apt to make a particular
appeal to me, and Scots poetry, in the higher range, pleasures
me like no other. Dunbar was quick to insist that he was a lesser
poet than Chaucer, but Dunbar's poetry speaks to me in ways
that Chaucer's never does and never could. It finds the familiar

in me. The language of Dunbar's poetry, and that of certain col-leagues writing five hundred years later, comes across as some-thing half-remembered, like a first language since superseded. When I arrive at Glasgow Central Station these days, a wave of recognition breaks over me as I step off the train. The speech in the air around me carries experiences which, though I may not have realized it till then, were obscured by the invisible wall that separates Scotland from England.

When I went south to live in London, at the age of thirty, I admit it, I did a Boswell. I straightened out my tongue. It had never been "abominable"—at least not since those adolescent days—but it had what others were pleased to refer to as a "lilt." When I heard myself speak on a tape recorder or on the radio, I would be surprised at how strong my accent was. But gradually it faded. It happened without my noticing. I didn't shoo it away, or plot my advancement among the London literati by honeying the knobbled surfaces and thistled joints of my syllables. I excuse this fact, when people remark on it (invariably to my annoyance), by telling myself that my voice is mimetic by nature, that my tendency is to sound like those by whom I wish to be understood, that my Scots voice hasn't gone away, it's just con-cealed beneath these southern clothes. Or thae suddron claes.

The paradox—our own family paradox—is that while my accent traveled southwards, that of my parents went back in the opposite direction. In recent years, my father, in particular, would announce "ah cannae thole it," usually in reference to a politician or something else that he found "a right scunner." He never talked like that in the days when I was being persecuted for the company I kept. He would have said of the politician "I can't stand him," that he found him annoying. In his last years, living at the lower fringe of the Highlands among people who speak a mild modern form of Scots, he found his vowel sounds drawn back to the streets where he had grown up—not that far, it so happens, from the stamping ground of my notorious Gorbals cronies. I noticed a certain self-consciousness as he modulated into this voice, often for my benefit, but also a pleasure, a relaxation, at being reacquainted with his older tongue.

My mother would have no qualms about sticking with the "Glasgow" way. But one day, during my father's last illness, when he responded to doctor's orders by failing to take his medicines when he should have, threatening to go out when he shouldn't, and generally behaving obstinately, she sat down in her usual chair with an air of great weariness and turned to me.

"*Thrawn*, I think is the word," she said. Her precision took me aback. Thrawn means, literally, twisted or crooked, but it has a more common figurative sense, which is not hard to see: difficult, stubborn. Thrawn was indeed the word. I believe I had never heard her use it before. She must have been saving it up.

As for Boswell, several years after his abomination of Mrs. Miller, he was back in London, having in the meantime returned to Scotland to marry and set himself up as a lawyer. An entry in the Journal, March 30, 1772, finds him in a Covent Garden coffee house with Johnson, contemplating the idea of moving his practice south for good (he never did) "Mr Johnson is not against it; and says my having any Scotch accent would be but for a little while." Here he gives himself away. Almost a decade after having seen off Mrs. Miller, despite his lessons in "pronunciation" from Thomas Sheridan, Jamie is still talking native.

# Footnotes to a Double Life

## Ariel Dorfman

I should not be here to tell this story.[1]

---

[1] That is how my memoir *Heading South, Looking North: A Bilingual Journey* began.

Begin, began, beginning: in a manner of speaking. Because it took me almost nine months to come up with that first line and the five or six lines that followed. It was, in fact, exactly nine, but I hesitate to say so, as this evokes an abusively glib parallel between gestation/childbirth and creation/writing. But nothing glib about the nine months of hard work, scribble, clack, *tecleo continuo,* day after day, *día y noche.* Writing and rewriting the first ten pages of the book over and over again until I wondered if my wife had been right to tell me that I would go insane before I had completed the first chapter.

Forget the many other reasons why self-scrutiny can be so agonizing and zero in on what was really bugging me: I couldn't for the life or death of me decide in which of my two languages to write the story of my life. They had been *disputándome* for most of my existence, each of them dominating my life monolingually, for long stretches of years freezing the other out of power and articulation. Until I got tired of being a child pulled this and pushed that way by two distraught parents insulting each other in a language the other pretended not to know but that the disputed offspring understood all too well. Tired of being a husband with two squabbling wives or a mistress with two lovers or maybe I was the bed where the two vocabularies coupled or . . . choose your metaphor, *tu metáfora.* What matters is that by the time I had decided to write the memoir, these two sides of my brain, these two tongues lodged in the cavity called my *cabeza*—also known as a head— had declared a truce, had decided to stop waging war because I needed them both to survive exile, to make a living (you get paid once in Spanish and once in English and between both payments, *sabes,* you manage to get one whole meal for one family of four). I needed them because of the dictatorship in Chile: how to deny the possibility of transmitting twice over to an increasingly deaf and indifferent world the story of my ravaged land—which would, presumably, lead to my being able to convince twice as many people. And that armistice led me to believe that I could now tackle the story of my life, I could at least give it an ending that did not conclude in strife and dividing walls.

But no sooner did I start to write the first sentences of that autobiography in one of the languages, say English, than the Spanish misbehaved abominably, blocked those words as if they were alien, an in flagrante case of linguistic adultery. And the same menace of divorce—"you do this, boy, and I am outta here"—if I tried to spin the tale in Spanish, my English telling me it would not tolerate such treachery. I am using a metaphor, of course. *Claro que sí.* Languages do not exist as characters in a play. They may talk about sex but they don't—you know—*do it*; talk about battles, but don't fire real bullets. By conferring an independent life on them, I am merely trying to express their extraordinary power over me, how I felt that their double boycott of my writing functioned in the most concrete of ways. *Muy simple.*

So how did this boycott work?

Whenever I wrote anything about my life, in either language, it simply sounded . . . false, *falso*, fraudulent, *fraudulento*. And the Spanish, by the way, has that *lento* adhered to its tail, that sense of a fraud that is slow, that persists, that prolongs itself inside your mind. And the English is, therefore, at least for me, peremptory and cutting, something not to be forgiven, that "t" at the end terminating all altercations. Nothing *lento* about my English language self. In a word (and there's the rub, it can't be expressed in a word at all, *ni en una palabra*): jealousy/*celos*, they paralyzed me by making me feel that anything I stated on paper in one language about the other would not pass the test.

So what was it that they actually objected to, my two *amantes*?

Each had agreed to allow the other right of passage, rites of passage, as long, I came to realize, *as long as the story being told was not theirs.* Spanish said: *yo voy a contar lo que pasó, porque me pasó a mí.* And English repeated (or anticipated first) the same words: I am the one who will tell what happened, because it happened to me. I could argue with each that it had happened to me, and therefore to both of them, to the two zones of poor me—but they argued back that it could be expressed first only by one rather than the other, because languages can incorporate any number of loans from another tongue, but at their moment of enunciation demand exclusivity. And so nine months went by. So desperate those months, so crippled by the certainty that I could not venture one word in either language without feeling that I was betraying one or the other. Because this was not a quick fling, it wasn't an article I wrote for the *New York Times* that had to be in English or one that I wrote for *El País* in Madrid that had to be in Spanish, a novel like *Konfidenz* that I penned in Spanish and then translated into English and then went back and corrected the Spanish version with what I had learnt while transposing it to my other tongue. Oh no, this was the far more serious matter of moving in, settling down, with one or with the other, choosing one over the other, giving it primacy, bragging dibs, establishing a hierarchy and *una primogenitura.* Favoring one over the other to tell the story of their troubled relationship. Imagine two countries at war who have fought each other to a standstill and find, at the moment of the armistice, that the final treaty will only be in one of the tongues. The next day they

It's that simple: there is a day in my past, a day many years ago in Santiago de Chile, when I should have died and did not.[2]

～

would be at war again, right? This time over whose language would be the one used to define the terms, the frontiers, the reparations, the repatriation of enemy soldiers. Otherwise, who knows what contumacious and abstruse clauses and particulars the rival entity has smuggled into the final draft.

I'll tell you how raving and frenzied I got: one dawn, after an almost sleepless night, I grabbed a pad of paper and scratched out some words in . . . French. C'est vrai! A language I can stutter, barely bring myself to write. You want neutral?, some worm in my brain asked. *Quieres neutralidad?* Well, you got it . . . Yes, that's what I got: an impartial arbiter to speak for me, but she (is French a she?, voluptuously so, I think) had no capacity for writing anything eloquent or intimate: so again, I had no memoir.

That madness at dawn may, however, have been what saved me. I had hit the bottom of the pit. I think it was the next morning (it certainly makes this a more interesting story if there is an immediate consequence) that I decided that enough was enough, *basta*, it was time to let my languages know who was in charge. If you do not let me decide, I said to them, I will end up in a mental institution and my words will be neither in English or Spanish but a combination of the two of you closer to sheer jarring gibberish.

For reasons that I prefer to keep under strict lock and key here inside, I then proceeded to choose English as the vehicle for my life, give English first rights—but temporarily, I promised, just to get this damn thing into the world; and then, I turned and murmured to my Spanish, *te voy a dejar que re-escribas por entero el libro*, I'll let you write your own version of my life.

It was a trap and maybe my Spanish knew it—or maybe at that time she, he, it, didn't care. Maybe she knew that once the story had been established in a certain way, once I had told it in English, it would be basically invariable.

Which turned out to be the case: my rewriting of the memoir in Spanish after I completed it in English followed the structure, story, explorations of history and of the mind which its rival language had set out. Spanish had to overflow its words inside the house that English built.

And yet, how changed was that house as it filled with Spanish.

It was not the same book.

[2] Look at the first lines in the Spanish text, read them: *"Si estoy contando esta historia, si la puedo contar, es porque alguien, muchos años atrás en Santiago de Chile, murió en mi lugar."* Meaning: "If I am writing this story, if I can tell it, it is because someone, many years ago in Santiago de Chile, died instead of me."

It took me a good few weeks to figure that one out, that I could not merely transfer and smooth the English words into Spanish, that Spanish was going to demand that I keep at least part of my promise and allow a slightly different version of my existence to circulate in the world.

That was the place, the house of death.[3] That's where I caught pneumonia one Saturday night in February of 1945, when my parents had gone out by themselves for the first time since we had arrived in the States—and I carefully use that verb, to catch,

---

See how the Spanish elongates and complicates the brief and unaffected early formulation (I should not be here to tell this story) of the English? Beginning with an If/ *Si*, making existence more conditional, adding a second if/*si* to vaguely suggest how halting this process has been. But more crucially: the Spanish required that from the very start I include the fact that someone had died in my place, instead of me. I could not remember my survival in Spanish without remembering immediately the Spanish-speaking person who was dead while I was alive. I had never spoken in English to the man, Claudio Jimeno, who died in my stead. He makes an appearance very soon in the English version of the memoir, of course, but not in the first lines. My Spanish, therefore, was not willing to leave aside or behind the community it carried inside its vowels and grammar, needed to thrust that reciprocal dimension of my life straight into the reader's mind. Without delay. Because this was my *historia*: not just my story, but my simultaneous history, the history I had both made and suffered. Not that I had blocked myself from spelling all this out in my English. My memoir is, among other things, an exploration of how we shape history as it shapes us, how a language speaks us as much as we speak it. But in the sensuous Spanish pounding out of the specific words, the emphasis was altered, the landscape found itself widened, it was established from the get-go that this story would not be mine alone. Someone else died. And the first words that someone heard in his life, the last words he heard in his life, the first and last words I said to him, to my friend Claudio, were in Spanish. The revolution he died for, that I did not give my life for, was lived by both of us, in the Spanish of Chile.

But this other version is also determined by what sounds better. "When I should have died and did not," well, that resonates in me dramatically, perhaps even elegantly, the way in which the succession of *d*s re-enforce one another, the way in which that *not* at the end closes any door to doubt. The Spanish translation *cuando debí haber muerto y no lo hice* is weak, awkwardly constructed, repeating the ugly *b*s (*debí haber*). Worse still, the use of the verb *hacer* (*hice*) misconstrues the original meaning in English, by positing the survival as more active than it really was. To give an approximate equivalent of the first sentence in the English language memoir I would have had to write something like *cuando la muerte vino por mí y no me encontró* ("when death came for me and did not find me"), but that is a thought and a structure of feeling I wanted to reserve for later in the text.

[3] We're already in the second chapter (I've been born into Spanish and Argentina and at a very young age am already being subjected to displacement in time and space), and I'm referring to my arrival in New York at the age of two and a half—speaking not a word of the language in which I write this footnote.

aware of its wild ambiguity, still unsure, even now, if that sickness invaded me or if I was the one who invited it in. But more of that later. To save his life, that boy was interned in a hospital, isolated in a ward where nobody spoke a word of Spanish. For three weeks, he saw his parents only on visiting days and then only from behind a glass partition.[4]

My parents have told me the story so often that sometimes I have the illusion that I am the one remembering, but that hope quickly fades, as when you arrive at a movie theater late and never discover what really happened, are forever at the mercy of those who have witnessed the beginning: *te internaron en ese hospital*, my mother says slowly, picking out the words as if for the first time, *no nos acordamos del nombre*,[5] there is a large glass wall, it is a cold bare white hospital ward, my parents have told me that every time they came to see me, tears streamed

---

[4] Note the change to the third person. Distance. My demon and my savior and my instrument: *distancia.* I am apparently already trying to compensate for the fact that this is my English language persona speaking about what happened to *él, that one, that kid, ese niño.*

I was not there—this Ariel who writes this in English now, who wrote that in English when I began the second chapter of the memoir. Is it the Spanish that, growling gently inside, demanded some signal in its direction, that nod to its past dominion? Maybe. But it turns out that Spanish itself did not know, does not remember, what happened next, has kept not one *pedacito* of *rememoranza,* is as orphaned as English—as the child himself felt himself to be . . . So the next line had to be: My parents have told me the story so often . . .

[5] And must have told it in Spanish, because that is how I recall their own memory, narrating me, my mother, into the future with the tongue that she herself had used to hijack a different identity from the Yiddish she had first heard floating over her infantile head as she headed from Europe to Argentina on that steamer from Hamburg four years before the First World War was to ravage her continent of birth.

But this is also a device—not merely stylistic—that I use throughout this memoir . . . and in some of my journalism as well as my later novels. Introduce Spanish directly into the text (or English if the text is in Spanish), often without explaining or trans-

down my face, that I tried to touch them, I watch myself watching my parents so near and so far away behind the glass, mouthing words in Spanish I can't hear. Then my mother and my father are gone and I turn and I am alone and my lungs hurt and I realize then, as I realize now, that I am very fragile, that life can snap like a twig. I realize this in Spanish and I look up and the only adults I see are nurses and doctors. They speak to me in a language I don't know. A language that I will later learn is called English. In what language do I respond? In what language can I respond?

Three weeks later, when my parents came to collect their son,[6] now sound in body but in all probability slightly insane in mind, I disconcerted them by refusing to answer their Spanish questions, by speaking only English. "I don't understand," my mother says that I said—and from that moment onward I stubbornly, steadfastly, adamantly refused to speak a word in the tongue I had been born into.

---

lating, no help to the reader, you're on your own, as I was, shipwrecked in a sea of words we don't understand. A tiny taste of what it means to be adrift in someone else's language. Or maybe, in this case, it is a way of assuaging the Spanish in which, after all, this event first happened and was first told, by giving it a token presence— letting it sit down at a remote corner of the table and not be submitted to translation's perfidious traffic.

A technique, by the way, that I first noticed in a number of Spanish American novels—for instance by the Peruvian José María Arguedas or the Paraguayan Augusto Roa Bastos. These authors, who came from bilingual societies (Quechua/ Spanish and Guaraní/Spanish, respectively), interjected many native words into the Spanish text and eliminated footnotes or glossaries, forcing their readers to infer the meaning from the context, refusing to let us off the hook. You don't understand? *No comprendes, carajo?* Too bad! Learn Guaraní!

[6] Here my devious double-crossing mind makes a transition, tries to have it both ways, find a middle ground between the Spanish in which this occurred and the English in which it is expressed: *my parents* and *their son*, an attempt to be object and subject.

I did not speak another word of Spanish for ten years.[7]

Out there,[8] at the edge of my tongue, within reach of the Spanish words I hardly knew how to formulate, a real challenge was

---

[7] Perhaps I can now elucidate the deepest reason why I chose to write that memoir in English. *Heading South, Looking North: A Bilingual Journey* is organized in two alternating series of chapters. One sequence starts by stating that I was almost killed in Santiago during the military coup of 1973 and goes on, in the ensuing chapters, to follow me as I survive death on several occasions until the day when I finally am able to go into exile, a situation that will force me to live away from Chile and therefore be bilingual. The other sequence starts with my birth in Argentina (my birth into Spanish) and, after a first chapter which ends with my switching from Spanish into English (the one I am commenting on here), proceeds to show how history finally sent me back to Latin America, to my native tongue, how the day when I could have died and did not was awaiting me in Chile. The central events that determine the two sequences are both traumatic, moments when death circled me, whether in the New York hospital as a child, or on the streets of Santiago as a young adult. And both these shattering events were lived by me in Spanish. So, why English?

I think it may have been because it was the best way of dealing with the ordeal, using the measured framework of the English words to contain the pain, to look at those circumstances in a sort of roundabout, indirect fashion. English as a sort of oblique mirror that allowed me to see the events in a different (or at least tolerable) light, work through this confession, show myself, perhaps reveal myself, use the distance, treat myself as an almost fictional object. So much so that very often, when, later on, I was reworking the text in Spanish, I would find myself sick and trembling, faint with anxiety, asking my book how I had dared to write this, what naked madness must I have gone through and tamed in order to finally bring out into the open such secret thoughts. And those events, after all, those two close encounters with death, were at the origin of my conversion to the English in which I was writing this; they were, in some bizarre manner, the mothers, *las madres* of this very language. Or maybe the *padres*, maybe the Spanish words had inseminated an English child in my brain. Whatever the gender, this much seems to be true: to unveil one's origins, to journey to where it all started, we may need to use a different tongue, create an alter ego and trust him with the furtive truth we have told no one. You can't journey to your origin without a translator of some sort by your side. And a consolation: the ultimate reconciliation of my languages in this memoir, perhaps in this commentary as I write it. The very fact that I can write it may be proof that they are finally beginning to trust one another.

[8] By now, I have been forced to leave the States and journey to Chile, forced to speak and write the detested Spanish language.

lying in wait for me: the people who spoke that language, the guardians of a plenitude of things and experiences that were to sensually surround my body and demand a name. That Spanish out there contained my future. It contained the words of García Lorca I would say to Angélica one day, *Verde que te quiero verde*, the lover-like green of desire, and the words of Quevedo I would say to my country, *Miré los muros de la patria mía*, watching the walls of my fatherland crumble, and the words of Neruda I would say to the revolution, *Sube a nacer conmigo, hermano*, rise and be born with me, my brother, and the words of Borges I would whisper to time, *los tigres de la memoria*, the tigers of memory with which I would try to fool death once again. I would realize one day that the word for hope in Spanish, the word *esperanza*, hides within its syllables the sound and meaning of *esperar*, to wait, that there was in the language itself a foretelling of frustration, a warning to be cautious, to hope but not to hope too much because the experience of those who forged those syllables tells them that we end up, more often than not, being violated by history.[9]

Not only wonders, in Spanish: also learning with it how to avoid responsibility. A day comes back to me—I must have been sixteen—the first time I realized that Spanish was beginning to speak me, had infiltrated my habits. It was in carpentry class and

---

[9] If I do not remember the first transition of my life (from non-language to Spanish) or the second one (from Spanish into English)—and have had to basically invent the way in which I experienced them—this return to Spanish is one that needs to be expressed as a real process. But that does not mean that I know exactly how that happened, that I was conscious, while it was happening, of what was going on. It was a long, drawn-out seduction, a back and forth operation, a crossing and recrossing of the borders of my own mind. And so I do not focus on one event as much as offer an approximation, anticipate a future when Spanish will be present in all its glory. As if it had been calling to me, *llamándome todos esos años de exilio*, during all those years of banishment.

I had given a final clumsy bang with a hammer to a monstrous misshapen contraption I had built and it broke, fell apart right there, so I turned to the carpentry teacher and "*Se rompió,*" I said, shrugging my shoulders.

His mouth had twisted in anger. "*Se, se, se,*" he hissed. "Everything in this country is *se,* it broke, it just happened, why in the hell don't you say I broke it, I screwed up. Say it, say, *Yo lo rompí, yo, yo, yo,* take responsibility, boy." And all of a sudden I was a Spanish speaker, I was being berated for having used that form of the language to hide behind, I had automatically used that ubiquitous, impersonal *se,* I had escaped into the language, *escapé lenguaje adentro,* merged with it.[10]

I became conscious then of the other elusive ways in which the language allowed its devoutest followers to pass the buck on to others, the proliferation of passive forms and the overemployment of the *hay que, había que, habría que* (approximately, "it should be necessary to . . .") which, in years to come, would drive me crazy, people all around me endlessly discussing in smoke-filled rooms what should be done and very few of them effectively doing anything. But by then I had gone deeper into the

---

[10] And here comes English to the rescue! The presence of that other language inside me, back then, and also now, does not allow me to hide as much as I would have wanted, as many of my compatriots can and still do. Not that English-language speakers are any less adept than those who practice Spanish at squirming out of accountability. Kissinger uses his (foreign-learned) English as skillfully as Pinochet uses his (barely learned) Spanish to avoid, both of them, facing the crimes they are alleged to have committed against humanity. Being bilingual does not exempt you from any of the horrors of the human. No one language condemns you to laziness or efficiency, mendacity or truth. If you dispose of two languages, therefore, you can lie twice as much—but also have a good extra whack at the truth, if you are so inclined.

language and learned that this multiplication of possibilities and parallel paths could also be a virtue, could also enrich the language. I had come to explore the verb system in Spanish, perhaps the richest in the Indo-European family of languages. I had come to adore the fluid use of time that Spanish plays with, I had internalized the subjunctive, to mentally live a plurality of forms of time that had not yet occurred, a time that was suspended and waiting to occur, a time that existed in the mind even if it had no chance of materializing in history, the construction of alternative imaginary universes always haunting the hard reality of our hearts trapped in the prison house of today and now and right here.[11]

I was not aware of what was happening to my mind: it was a subtle, cunning, camouflaged process, the vocabulary and the grammatical code seeping into my consciousness slowly, turning me into a person who, without acknowledging it, began to function in either language. Although from the very beginning I did not allow my new language to enter into a dialogue with the older one. I stubbornly avoided comparing their relative merits, what one could offer me that the other could not. It was as if they inhabited two strictly different, segregated zones in my mind, or perhaps as if there were two Edwards,[12] one for each

---

[11] The language I wrote my memoir in may be English, but the aesthetic seems to be resolutely Spanish American, the creation of that parallel conjuring up of what might have been, what still might be, language as the one irrevocable site of freedom, my life as not only what happened, but what almost happened. Life as a series of footnotes to a text written by someone else, more powerful, apparently in command. Latinos: embracing our margins as if we had chosen them instead of history imposing that marginality upon us.

[12] In my insanity to become American and leave my Spanish past behind, I had rebaptized myself Edward. The few friends I have left over from adolescence still call me Ed.

language, each incommunicado like a split personality, each trying to ignore the other, afraid of contamination. I did not attempt—
or even contemplate the possibility of—cross-fertilization: to
weigh the caliber and performance of one against the other
would have meant creating a territory from which to think the
phenomenon, a common space they both shared within me. It
would have meant admitting that I was irrevocably bilingual,
opening the door to questions of identity that I was much too
vulnerable and immature to face: Who is it that speaks Spanish?
Is it the same youngster who speaks English? Is there a core
that is unchanged no matter what dictionary you reach for?
And which is better equipped to tell a particular story? And
how is it that your body language changes when you switch
from one to the other? Is it a different body? Questions that
only many years later, only now that I have agreed to their
coexistence, can I begin to register.[13] Questions which, if I had
asked them when I was first starting this journey toward duality,
would have made me clamp down, suffocate Spanish again,

---

[13] Most of this paragraph was not in the original manuscript. John Glusman, my
friend and editor at Farrar, Straus, believed that I needed, at some point in
my memoir, to examine these problems. How did I do it? What does it mean to be,
feel, live bilingually? At what point does Spanish take over, when does English con-
cede? How in the hell did it, does it, actually *happen*?

And what I wrote then, in response to his legitimate questions, was as far as I
could go, at least back then. Back then? Even now I do not dare to venture any
deeper into that territory.

As if the reader had not already realized that this collaboration between my two
languages, my two loves, is a precarious and fragile one, that can be all too easily
upset. Dangerous, certain questions. Like a sweetheart asking if she makes love
better than the other one, the wife, the legitimate spouse.

I am wary of opening up anything that could disturb the balance I have somehow
struck between my two recently reconciled but still potentially antagonistic vocabularies. There is someone inside me that makes the decision about when to speak
Spanish and when to speak English. Frequently, most of the time, this is decided

deny its right to a voice. And my Spanish knew this, and cooperated, was glad to be once again inside my head, did not call attention to its gains, was not stupidly going to let itself crow victory when suddenly, in the middle of a sentence in English, a word in Spanish would make its upstart appearance as if nothing was more natural in the world, given that there was no English equivalent for that untranslatable turn of phrase. My Spanish did not demand that I examine why I needed that precise word when I had an infinitude of English at my tongue's end, why it was irreplaceable. Having smuggled itself in, my Spanish was wise enough not to corner me. Instead, quite simply, it grew. And grew. And grew.[14]

---

for me. I answer, generally, in the language in which I am addressed: I sit at the computer and set the language for Spanish if I am writing for *Revista Proceso* in Mexico or reach for the English book of synonyms if I am planning to publish the piece in the *Washington Post*; I use Spanish with my graduate students and English with my undergrads—and so on and so forth, *y así es la cosa*. But there are many solitary moments in my day, inevitably, for any author, when I am left alone with *mis dos idiomas,* and I have to decide which of them will receive my full attention. And I do not intend, for the moment, to ask myself how I reach that conclusion, why one at a certain moment sprints out of my fingers onto the keyboard or simmers to the surface when I am looking at a tree during a walk through the woods. I don't want to know, I don't want to legislate, I don't want it to be anything other than spontaneous, automatic, surfacing from some depth that I prefer not to gaze into.

[14] This much I do know. It is still growing. As is the English. Even when I do not use one of the two languages, when one of them is relegated to the attic of my life, that language, be it English or Spanish, continues to grow—and reign. At this very moment, as I compose this, my Spanish is whispering instructions, suggestions, blowing rhythms my way, shaping the rival's choices. Creating between the two of them, something that is not quite one hundred percent English or Spanish, but something quite other, *creciendo ambos*. I swear it is true, I hope it is true. *Juro que es cierto.*
*Más bien: espero que sea cierto.*

# *My Yiddish*

## Leonard Michaels

In Paris one morning in the seventies, walking along rue Mahler, I saw a group of old men in an argument, shouting and gesticulating. I wanted to know what it was about, but my graduate school French was good enough only to read great writers, not good enough for an impassioned argument or even conversation with the local grocer. But then, as I walked by the old men, I felt a shock and a surge of exhilaration. I did understand them. My god, I possessed the thing—spoken French! Just as suddenly, I crashed. The old men, I realized, were shouting in Yiddish.

Like a half-remembered dream, the incident lingered. It seemed intensely personal, yet impersonal. Meaning had come alive in me. I hadn't translated what the old men said. I hadn't done anything. A light turned on. Where nothing had been, there was something.

Philosophers used to talk about The Understanding as if it were a distinct mental function. Today they talk about epistemology or cognitive science. As for The Understanding, it's acknowledged in IQ tests, the value of which is subject to debate. It's also acknowledged in daily life in countless informal ways. You're on the same wave length with others or you are not. The Paris incident, where I rediscovered The Understanding, made me wonder if Descartes's remark, "I think, therefore I am," might be true in his case, but not mine. I prefer to say, "I am, therefore I think." And also, therefore, I speak.

Until I was five, I spoke only Yiddish. It did much to permanently qualify my thinking. Eventually I learned to speak English, then to imitate thinking as it transpires among English speakers. To some extent, my intuitions and my expression of thoughts remain basically Yiddish. I can say only approximately how this is true. For example this joke:

> The rabbi says, "What's green, hangs on the wall, and whistles?"
> The student says, "I don't know."
> The rabbi says, "A herring."
> The student says, "Maybe a herring could be green and hang on the wall, but it absolutely doesn't whistle."
> The rabbi says, "So it doesn't whistle."

The joke is inherent in Yiddish, not any other language. It's funny, and, like a story by Kafka, it isn't funny. I confess that I don't know every other language. Maybe there are such jokes in Russian or Chinese, but no other language has a history like Yiddish, which, for ten centuries, has survived the dispersion and murder of its speakers.

As the excellent scholar and critic Benjamin Harshav points out, in *The Meaning of Yiddish,* the language contains many words that don't mean anything—*nu, epes, tockeh, shoyn.* These are fleeting interjections, rather like sighs. They suggest, without meaning anything, "so," "really," "well," "already." Other Yiddish words and phrases, noticed by Harshav, are meaningful but defeat translation. Transparent and easy to understand, how-

ever, is the way Yiddish serves speech—between you and me—
rather than the requirements of consecutive logical discourse;
that is, between the being who goes by your name and who
speaks to others objectively and impersonally. For example, five
times five is twenty-five, and it doesn't whistle.

Yiddish is probably at work in my written English. This
moment, writing in English, I wonder about the Yiddish undercurrent. If I listen, I can almost hear it: "This moment"—a stress
followed by two neutral syllables—introduces a thought which
hangs like a herring in the weary droop of "writing in English,"
and then comes the announcement, "I wonder about the Yiddish undercurrent." The sentence ends in a shrug. Maybe I hear
the Yiddish undercurrent, maybe I don't. The sentence could
have been written by anyone who knows English, but it probably
would not have been written by a well-bred Gentile. It has too
much drama, and might even be disturbing, like music in a
restaurant or an elevator. The sentence obliges you to abide in
its staggered flow, as if what I meant were inextricable from my
feelings and required a lyrical note. There is a kind of enforced
intimacy with the reader. A Jewish kind, I suppose. In Sean
O'Casey's lovelier prose you hear an Irish kind.

Wittgenstein says in his *Philosophical Investigations*, "Aren't
there games we play in which we make up the rules as we go
along, including this one." *Nu*. Any Yiddish speaker knows that.
A good example of playing with the rules might be Montaigne's
essays, the form that people say he invented. *Shoyn*, a big inven-
tor. Jews have always spoken essays. The scandal of Montaigne's
essays is that they have only an incidental relation to a consecutive logical argument but they are cogent nonetheless. Their
shape is their sense. It is determined by motions of his mind and

feelings, not by a pretension to rigorously logical procedure. Montaigne literally claims his essays are himself. Between you and him nothing intervenes. A Gentile friend used to say, in regard to writing she didn't like, "There's nobody home." You don't have to have Jewish ancestors, like those of Montaigne and Wittgenstein, to understand what she means.

I didn't speak English until I was five because my mother didn't speak English. My father had gone back to Poland to find a wife. He returned with an attractive seventeen-year-old who wore her hair in a long black braid. Men would hit on her, so my father wouldn't let her go take English classes. She learned English by doing my elementary school homework with me. As for me, before and after the age of five, I was susceptible to lung diseases and spent a lot of time in a feverish bed, in a small apartment on the Lower East Side of Manhattan, where nobody spoke anything but Yiddish. Years passed before I could ride a bike or catch a ball. In a playground fight, a girl could have wiped me out. I was badly coordinated and had no strength or speed, only a Yiddish mouth.

For a long time, Yiddish was my whole world. In this world family didn't gather before dinner for cocktails and conversation. There were no cocktails, but conversation was daylong and it included criticism, teasing, opinionating, gossiping, joking. It could also be very gloomy. To gather before dinner for conversation would have seemed unnatural. I experienced the pleasure of such conversation for the first time at the University of Michigan, around 1956. It was my habit to join a friend at his apartment after classes. He made old fashioneds and put music on the phonograph, usually chamber music. By the time we left for dinner, I felt uplifted by conversation and splendid music. Mainly, I was drunk, also a new experience. Among my Jews, conversation had no ritual character, no aesthetic qualities. I never learned to cultivate the sort of detachment that allows for the always potentially offensive personal note. Where I came from, everything was personal.

From family conversation I gathered that, outside of my Yiddish child-world, there were savages who didn't have much to say but could fix the plumbing. They were fond of animals, liked to go swimming, loved to drink and fight. All their problems were solved when they *hut geharget yiddin*. Killed Jews. Only the last has been impossible for me to dismiss. Like many other people I have fixed my own plumbing, owned a dog and a cat, gotten drunk, etc., but everything in my life, beginning with English, has been an uncertain movement away from my *hut geharget* Yiddish childhood. When a BBC poet said he wanted to shoot Jews on the West Bank, I thought, "*Epes*. What else is new?" His righteousness, his freedom to say it, suggests that he believes he is merely speaking English, and antisemitism is a kind of syntax, or what Wittgenstein calls "a form of life." But in fact there is something new, or anyhow more evident lately. The *geharget yiddin* disposition now operates at a remove. You see it in people who become hysterical when they feel that their ancient right to hate Jews is brought into question. To give an example would open a boxcar of worms.

It's possible to talk about French without schlepping the historical, cultural, or national character of a people into consideration. You cannot talk that way about Yiddish unless you adopt a narrow scholarly focus, or restrict yourself to minutiae of usage. The language has flourished in a number of countries. Theoretically, it has no territorial boundary. The meaning of Yiddish, in one respect, is No Boundaries. In another respect, for "a people without a land," the invisible boundaries couldn't be more clear. There is mutual contempt between what are called "universalist Jews" and Jewish Jews. It's an old situation. During the centuries of the Spanish Inquisition, Jews turned on Jews. In Shakespeare's *The Merchant of Venice*—assuming the merchant Antonio is a gay converso, or new Christian, and Shylock is an Old Testament moralistic Jewish Jew—the pound of flesh, a grotesquely exaggerated circumcision, is to remind Antonio (who says, "I know not why I am so sad") of his origins.

The first time I went to a baseball game, the great slugger Hank Greenberg, during warm-up, casually tossed a ball into the stands, a gift to the crowd of pre-adolescent kids among whom I sat. My hand, thrusting up in a blossom of hands, closed on that baseball. I carried it home, the only palpable treasure I'd ever owned. I never had toys. On Christmas nights I sometimes dreamed of waking and finding toys in the living room. *Tokeh?* Yes, really. If there is a support group for Christmas depressives, I will be your leader. The baseball made me feel like a real American. It happened to me long before I had a romance with the mythical blond who grants citizenship to Jews. By then I was already fifteen. I had tasted *traif* and long ago stopped speaking Yiddish except when I worked as a waiter in Catskills hotels. What Yiddish remained was enough to understand jokes, complaints, insults, and questions. As guests entered the dining room, a waiter might say, "Here come the *vildeh chayes*," or wild animals. One evening in the Catskills I went to hear a political talk, given in Yiddish. I understood little except that Yiddish could be a language of analysis, spoken by intellectuals. I felt alienated and rather ashamed of myself for not being like them.

Family members could speak Polish as well as Yiddish, and some Hebrew and Russian. My father worked for a short while in Paris and could manage French. My mother had gone to high school in Poland and was fluent in Polish, but refused to speak the language even when I asked her to. Her memory of pogroms made it unspeakable. In Yiddish and English I heard about her father, my grandfather, a tailor who made uniforms for Polish army officers. Once, after he'd worked all night to finish a uniform, the officer wouldn't pay. My grandfather, waving a pair of scissors, threatened to cut the uniform to pieces. The officer paid. The Germans later murdered my grandfather, his wife, and one daughter. Polish officers imprisoned in Katyn forest and elsewhere were massacred by Stalin. This paragraph, beginning with the first sentence and concluding with a moral, is in the form of a *geshichte,* or Yiddish story, except that it's in English and merely true.

At the center of my Yiddish, lest I have yet failed to make myself clear, remains *hut geharget yiddin,* from which, like the disgorged contents of a black hole in the universe, come the jokes, the thinking, the meanings, and the meaninglessness. In 1979, American writers were sent to Europe by the State Department. I went to Poland and gave talks in Warsaw, Poznan, and Cracow. I was surprised by how much seemed familiar, and exceedingly surprised by the intelligence and decency of the Poles, a few of whom became friends and visited me later in America. One of the Poles whom I didn't see again was a woman in Cracow with beautiful blue eyes and other features very like my mother's. I was certain that she was a Jew though she wore a cross. I didn't ask her questions. I didn't want to know her story. I could barely look at her. I detest the word "shiksa," which I've heard used more often by friendly antisemites than Jews, but in my personal depths it applies to her.

As suggested earlier, in Yiddish there is respect for meaninglessness. If the woman in Cracow was passing as a Catholic, was she therefore a specter of meaninglessness who haunted me, the child of Polish Jews, passing as an American writer? A familiar saying comes to mind, "If you forget you are a Jew, a Gentile will remind you," but, in the way of forgetting, things have gone much further. Lately, it might take a Jew to remind a Jew that he or she is a Jew. Then there is a risk of ruining the friendship. For an extreme example, I have had depressing arguments with Jewish Stalinists who, despite evidence from numerous and unimpeachable sources that Stalin murdered Jews because they were Jews, remain Stalinists. It's as if they would rather die than let personal identity spoil their illusions. Thus, the Jewish face of insanity says to me, "Stalin was a good guy. He just got a bad rap." A demonic parallel to this mentality is in the way Nazis used material resources, critical to their military effort, to murder Jews even as the Russian army was at the gates. They would rather die etc. In the second century, Tertullian, a father of the Christian church, insisted that absurdity is critical to belief. His political sophistication seems to me breathtaking, and also frightening in its implications. As the believers multiply everywhere, it becomes harder to believe—rationally—in almost anything.

Paradox as a cognitive mode is everywhere in Yiddish. It's probably in the genes and may explain the Jewish love of jokes. The flight from sense to brilliance effects an instant connection with listeners. Hobbes calls laughter "sudden glory," which is a superb phrase, but I've seen the Jewish comics, Lenny Bruce and Myron Cohen, reduce a nightclub audience to convulsive and inglorious agonies of laughter. When I worked in the Catskills hotels I noticed that it was often the *tumler*, or the hotel comic and hell raiser, to whom women abandoned themselves. Jerry Lewis, formerly a *tumler*, said in a televised interview that at the height of his fame he "had four broads a day." As opposed to Jerry Lewis, Hannah Arendt preferred disconnection. She used the snobbish word "banal" to describe the murderer of millions of Jews, and later said in a letter that despite the abuse she had received for using that word, she remained "light hearted."

Family was uncles and aunts who escaped from Poland and immigrated to the United States. They stayed with us until they found their own apartments. I'd wake in the morning and see small Jews sleeping on the living room floor. My Aunt Molly, long after she had a place of her own, often stayed overnight and slept on the floor. She was very lonely. Her husband was dead, her children had families of their own. A couch with a sheet, blanket, and pillow was available, but she refused such comforts. She wanted to be less than no trouble. She wore two or three dresses at once, almost her entire wardrobe. She slept on the floor in her winter coat and dresses. To see Molly first thing in the morning, curled against a wall, didn't make us feel good. She was the same height as my mother, around five feet, and had a beautiful intelligent melancholy face. I never saw her laugh, though she might chuckle softly, and she smiled when she teased me. She used to *krotz* (scratch) my back as I went to sleep, and she liked to speak to me in rhymes. First they were entirely Yiddish. Then English entered the rhymes.

*Label, gay fressen.*
*A fish shtayt on de tish.*

*Lenny, go eat.*
*A fish is on the table.*

*Shtayt* doesn't exactly mean "is." "Stands on the table" or "stays on the table" or "exists on the table" would be somewhat imprecise, though I think "A fish exists on the table" is wonderful. I once brought a girlfriend home, and Aunt Molly said, very politely, "You are looking very fit." Her "fit" sounded like "fet," which suggested "fat." My girlfriend squealed in protest. It took several minutes to calm her down. The pronunciation of "fet" for "fit" is typical of Yiddishified-English, which is almost a third language. I speak it like a native when telling jokes. The audience for such jokes has diminished over the years because most Jews now are politically liberal and have college degrees and consider such jokes undignified or racist. A joke that touches on this development tells of Jewish parents who worry about a son who studies English literature at Harvard. They go to see Kittredge, the great Shakespeare scholar, and ask if he thinks their son's Yiddish accent is a disadvantage. Kittredge booms, "Vot ekcent?"

As a child I knew only one Jew who was concerned to make a *bella figura*. He was a highly respected doctor, very handsome, always dressed in a fine suit and, despite his appearance, fluent in Yiddish. His office was in the neighborhood. He came every morning to my father's barber shop for a shave. A comparable miracle was the chicken-flicker down the block, a boisterous man who yelled at customers in vulgar funny Yiddish. This man's son was a star at MIT. In regard to such miracles, an expression I often heard was "He is up from pushcarts." It means he went from the Yiddish immigrant poverty to money or, say, a classy professorship. The day of such expressions is past. In the sixties there were Jewish kids who, as opposed to the spirit of Irving Howe's *The World of Our Fathers*, yelled, "Kill the parents." The suicidal implication is consistent with the paradoxical Yiddish they no longer spoke.

If I dressed nicely to go out, my mother would ask why I was *fapitzed*, which suggests "tarted up." Yiddish is critical of pretensions to being better than a Jew, and also critical of everything else. A man wants to have sex or wants to pee—what a scream. A woman appears naked before her husband and says, "I haven't got a thing to wear." He says, "Take a shave. You look like a bum." Henry Adams speaks of "derisive Jew laughter." It is easy to find derision produced by Jews, but Adams's word, aside from its stupid viciousness, betrays the self-hate and fear that inspires antisemitism among the educated, not excluding Jews. Ezra Pound called his own antisemitic ravings "stupid." The relation of stupidity and evil has long been noted.

Jewish laughter has a liberal purview and its numerous forms, some very silly, seem to me built into Yiddish. Sometime around puberty, I decided to use shampoo rather than handsoap to wash my hair. I bought a bottle of Breck. My father noticed and said in Yiddish, "Nothing but the best." I still carry his lesson in my heart, though I have never resumed using handsoap instead of shampoo. What has this to do with Yiddish? In my case, plenty, since it raises the question, albeit faintly, "Who do you think you are?"

What I have retained of Yiddish, I'm sorry to say, isn't much above the level of my Aunt Molly's poems. But what good to me is Yiddish? Recently, in Rome, during the High Holidays, a cordon was established around the synagogue in the ghetto, guarded by the police and local Jews. As I tried to pass I was stopped by a Jew. I was amazed. Couldn't he tell? I said, "Ich bin

a yid. Los mir gayen arein." He said, "Let me see your passport."
*La mia madrelingua* wasn't his. This happened to me before
with Moroccan Jews in France. I've wondered about Spinoza.
His Latin teacher was German, and the first Yiddish newspaper
was published in Amsterdam around the time of his death. Did
he know Yiddish?

I'm sure of very little about what I know except that the Yiddish I can't speak is more natural to my being than English, and
partly for that reason I've studied English poets. There is a line
in T. S. Eliot where he says words slip, slide, crack or something.
"Come off it, Tom," I think. "With words you never had no problem." Who would suspect from his hateful remark about a Jew in
furs that Eliot's family, like my mother's ancestors in Vienna, was
up from the fur business? Eliot liked Groucho Marx, a Jew, but
did he wonder when writing *Four Quartets,* with its striking allu-
sions to Saint John of the Cross, that the small dark brilliant
mystical monk might have been a Jew?

"Let there be light" are the first spoken words in the Old Testament. This light is understanding, not merely seeing. The Yiddish saying, "To kill a person is to kill a world," means the person
is no longer the embodiment, or a mode of the glorious nothing
that is the light, or illuminated world. This idea, I believe, is
elaborated in Spinoza's *Ethics.* Existence—or being—entails ethics.
Maybe the idea is also in Wittgenstein, who opens the *Tractatus*
this way: "The world is everything that is the case." So what is
the case? If it's the case that facts are bound up with values, it
seems Yiddish or Spinozist. Possibly for this reason Jewish writers in English don't write about murder as well as Christians.
Even Primo Levi, whose great subject is murder, doesn't offer
the lacerating specificity one might expect.

In regard to my own writing, its subterranean Yiddish keeps

me from being good at killing characters. The closest I've come is a story called "Trotsky's Garden," where I adopt a sort of Yiddish intonation to talk about his life. I'd read a psychological study that claimed Trotsky was responsible for murders only to please Lenin, his father figure. If so, his behavior was even worse than I'd thought. I wrote my story out of disappointment. I had wanted to admire Trotsky for his brilliant mind, courage, and extraordinary literary gifts. His description of mowing wheat in his diaries, for example, almost compares with Tolstoy's description of the same thing in *Anna Karenina*. Yiddish can be brutal, as, for example, *Gay koken aff yam,* which means "Go shit in the ocean," but in regard to murder what Jew compares with Shakespeare, Webster, Mark Twain, Flannery O'Connor, Cormac McCarthy, or Elmore Leonard? The Old Testament story of Abraham and Isaac, which is of profound importance to three faiths, stops short of murder, but it is relevant to the children in contemporary religious terrorism.

A story by Bernard Malamud begins with the death of a father whose name is Ganz. In Yiddish, "ganz" means "all" or "the whole thing" or "everything." Metaphorically, with the death of Ganz, the whole world dies. Everything is killed. Malamud couldn't have named the father Ganz if he had written the story in Yiddish. It would be too funny and undermine all seriousness. The death of a father, or a world-killed-in-a-person, is the reason for Hamlet's excessive grief, a condition feared among Jews for a reason given in the play: "All the uses of this world seem to me weary, stale, flat, and unprofitable." Because Hamlet Senior is dead, Hamlet Junior is as good as dead. Early in the play he jokes about walking into his grave, and the fifth act opens, for no reason, with Hamlet in a graveyard, and then he actually jumps into a grave. On the subject of grief, in "Mourning and Melancholia," Freud follows Shakespeare. Like Hamlet, who demands that his mother look at the picture of his father, Freud makes a great deal of the residual, or cathectic, force of an image. Again, regarding my Yiddish, when I once wrote about my father's death, I restricted my grief to a few images and a simple lamentation: "He gave. I took." My short sentences are self-critical, and have no relation to the work of writers known for short sentences. They are only Yiddish terseness seizing an English equivalent.

Shakespeare's short sentences—like "Let it come down," "Ripeness is all," "Can Fulvia die?"—seem to me amazing. I couldn't write one of those. This confession brings a joke instantly to mind. The synagogue's janitor is beating his breast and saying, "Oh, Lord, I am nothing." He is overheard by the rabbi who says, "Look who is nothing." Both men are ridiculed. A Jewish writer has to be careful. Between schmaltz and irony there is just an itty bitty step.

My mother sometimes switches in midsentence, when talking to me, from English to Yiddish. If meaning can leave English and reappear in Yiddish, does it have an absolutely necessary relation to either language? Linguists say, "No. Anything you can say in German you can say in Swahili which is increasingly Arabic." But no poet could accept the idea of linguistic equivalence, and a religious fanatic might want to kill you for proposing it. Ultimately, I believe, meaning has less to do with language than with music, a sensuous flow that becomes language only by default, so to speak, and by degrees. In great fiction and poetry, meaning is obviously close to music. Writing about a story by Gogol, Nabokov says it goes la, la, do, la la la etc. The story's meaning is radically musical. I've often had to rewrite a paragraph because the sound was wrong. When at last it seemed right, I discovered—incredibly—the sense was right. Sense follows sound. Otherwise we couldn't speak so easily or quickly. If someone speaks slowly, and sense unnaturally precedes sound, the person can seem too deliberative; emotionally false, boring. I can tell stories all day, but to write one that sounds right entails labors of indefinable innerness until I hear the thing I must hear before it is heard by anyone else. A standard of rightness probably exists for me in my residual subliminal Yiddish. Its effect is to inhibit as well as to liberate. An expression popular not long ago, "I hear you," was intended to assure you of being understood personally, as if there were a difference in comprehension between hearing and really hearing. In regard to being *really* heard, there are things in Yiddish that can't be heard in English. *Hazar fisl kosher.* "A pig has clean feet." It is an expression of contempt for hypocrisy. The force is in Yiddish concision. A pig is not clean. With clean feet it is even less clean. Another example: I was talking to a friend about a famous, recently deceased writer. The friend said, "He's *ausgespielt.*" Beyond dead. He's played out. So forget it. Too much has been said about him.

Cultural intuitions, or forms or qualities of meaning, dancing about in language, derive from the unique historical experience of peoples. The intuitions are not in dictionaries but carried by tones, gestures, nuances effected by word order, etc. When I understood the old men in Paris I didn't do or intend anything. It wasn't a moment of romantic introspection. I didn't know what language I heard. I didn't understand that I understood. What comes to mind is the assertion that begins the Book of John: "In the beginning was the word." A sound, a physical thing, the word is also mental. So this monism can be understood as the nature of everything. Like music that is the meaning of stories, physical and mental are aspects of each other. Yiddish, with its elements of German, Hebrew, Aramaic, Latin, Spanish, Polish, Russian, Rumanian, is metaphorically everything. A people driven hither and yon, and obliged to assimilate so much, returned immensely more to the world. How they can become necessary to murder is the hideous paradox of evil.

When I was five years old, I started school in a huge gloomy Victorian building where nobody spoke Yiddish. It was across the street from Knickerbocker Village, the project in which I lived. To cross that street meant going from love to hell. I said nothing in the classroom and sat apart and alone, and tried to avoid the teacher's evil eye. Eventually, she decided that I was a moron, and wrote a letter to my parents saying I would be transferred to the "ungraded class" where I would be happier and could play ping-pong all day. My mother couldn't read the letter so she showed it to our neighbor, a woman from Texas named Lynn Nations. A real American, she boasted of Indian blood, though she was blond and had the cheekbones, figure, and fragility of a fashion model. She would ask us to look at the insides of her teeth, and see how they were cupped. To Lynn this proved descent from original Americans. She was very fond of me, though we had no conversation, and I spent hours in her apartment looking at her art books and eating forbidden foods. I could speak to her husband, Arthur Kleinman, yet another furrier, and a lefty union activist, who knew Yiddish.

Lynn believed I was brighter than a moron and went to the school principal, which my mother would never have dared to do, and demanded an intelligence test for me. Impressed by her

Katharine Hepburn looks, the principal arranged for a school psychologist to test me. Afterwards, I was advanced to a grade beyond my age with several other kids, among them a boy named Bonfiglio and a girl named Estervez. I remember their names because we were seated according to our IQ scores. Behind Bonfiglio and Estervez was me, a kid who couldn't even ask permission to go to the bathroom. In the higher grade I had to read and write and speak English. It happened virtually overnight so I must have known more than I knew. When I asked my mother about this she said, "Sure you knew English. You learned from trucks." She meant: while lying in my sickbed I would look out the window at trucks passing in the street; studying the words written on their sides, I taught myself English. Unfortunately, high fevers burned away most of my brain, so I now find it impossible to learn a language from trucks. A child learns any language at incredible speed. Again, in a metaphorical sense, Yiddish is the language of children wandering for a thousand years in a nightmare, assimilating languages to no avail.

I remember the black shining print of my first textbook, and my fearful uncertainty as the meanings came with all their exotic Englishness and devoured what had previously inhered in my Yiddish. Something remained indigestible. What it is can be suggested, in a Yiddish style, by contrast with English. A line from a poem by Wallace Stevens, which I have discussed elsewhere, seems to me quintessentially goyish, or antithetical to Yiddish:

*It is the word* pejorative *that hurts.*

Stevens affects detachment from his subject, which is the poet's romantic heart, by playing on a French construction: "word *pejo-*

rative," like *mot juste,* makes the adjective follow the noun. Detachment is further evidenced in the rhyme of "word" and "hurts." The delicate resonance gives the faint touch of hurtful impact without obliging the reader to suffer the experience. The line is ironically detached even from detachment. In Yiddish there is plenty of irony, but not so nicely mannered or sensitive to a reader's experience of words. Stevens's line would seem too self-regarding; and the luxurious subtlety of his sensibility would seem unintelligible, if not ridiculous. He flaunts sublimities here, but it must be said that elsewhere he is as visceral and concrete as any Yiddish speaker.

I've lost too much of my Yiddish to know exactly how much remains. Something remains. A little of its genius might be at work in my sentences, but this has nothing to do with me personally. The pleasures of complexity and the hilarity of idiocy, as well as an idea of what's good or isn't good, are in Yiddish. If it speaks in my sentences, it isn't I, let alone me, who speaks.

When asked what he would have liked to be if he hadn't been born an Englishman, Lord Palmerston said, "An Englishman." The answer reminds me of a joke. A Jew sees himself in a mirror after being draped in a suit by a high-class London tailor. The tailor asks what's wrong. The Jew says, crying, "Vee lost de empire." The joke assimilates the insane fury that influenced the nature of Yiddish and makes it apparent that identity for a Jew is not, as for Palmerston, a witty preference.

# About the Contributors

LOUIS BEGLEY lives in New York City. His seventh novel, *Shipwreck*, was published in September 2003 by Alfred A. Knopf.

JAMES CAMPBELL worked as a printer in Glasgow, before going on to university in Edinburgh. Between 1978 and 1982, he was the editor of the literary quarterly *New Edinburgh Review*. His books include *Invisible Country: A Journey through Scotland* (1984), *Talking at the Gates: A Life of James Baldwin* (1991), and *This Is the Beat Generation* (2001). He lives in London, where he works for the *Times Literary Supplement*.

ARIEL DORFMAN, the Chilean expatriate writer and human rights activist, holds the Walter Hines Page Chair at Duke University. His books, written both in Spanish and English, have been translated into over thirty languages, his plays staged in more than one hundred countries. He has received numerous international awards, including the Danish ALOA prize for best foreign book (*Heading South, Looking North*) and the Laurence Olivier Award (for the play *Death and the Maiden*). His novels include *Widows, Konfidenz, The Nanny and the Iceberg*, and *Blake's Therapy*. His latest works include poetry (*In Case of Fire in a Foreign Land*), a new play (*Purgatory*), and a travel book (*Desert Memories*).

M. J. FITZGERALD is Director of the Creative Writing Program at the University of Minnesota and lives in Minneapolis with her partner,

Brian, and son, Robert. Her most recent story, "The Invention of Greek Statues," was published in *Literary Imagination,* the review of the Association of Literary Scholars and Critics.

HA-YUN JUNG's writing has appeared in various publications including *Prairie Schooner, The Threepenny Review,* the *New York Times,* and *Best New American Voices 2001.* She has received fiction fellowships from the University of Wisconsin-Madison and the Radcliffe Institute for Advanced Study and also a translation grant from the Korean Literature Translation Institute. After living in the United States for seven years, she recently returned to Korea, where she is at work on a novel.

BERT KEIZER works as a geriatrician and writer in Amsterdam. In 1994 he published his first book, *Het Refrein is Hein,* which he translated, or rather rewrote in English, under the title *Dancing with Mister D.* He has also written a novel about his work as a doctor in Africa and an appraisal of Wittgenstein. In the Netherlands he writes a weekly column in a national daily; in the United States, he appears regularly in *The Threepenny Review.* He is presently engaged in translating a selection of Emily Dickinson's letters into Dutch, an effort which by its very nature will go entirely unnoticed in the English-speaking world.

THOMAS LAQUEUR was born in Istanbul, Turkey, on September 6, 1945, and grew up in Beckley, West Virginia. He graduated from Swarthmore College in 1967 and received a Ph.D. in history from Princeton in 1973. Since then he has taught at Berkeley. He writes regularly on history and culture for the *London Review of Books,* the *Times Literary Supplement,* and other publications. His books include *Making Sex: Body from the Greeks to Freud* (which has been translated into over a dozen languages) and *Solitary Sex: A Cultural History of Masturbation.* He is now at work on a new project called *The Dead Among the Living.*

LEONARD MICHAELS was born in New York in 1933. He taught for many years in the English Department at the University of California, Berkeley, and after his retirement he divided his time between California and Italy. His books of fiction and nonfiction include *Going Places, I Would Have Saved Them If I Could, The Men's Club, Shuffle, Sylvia, To Feel These Things,* and *A Girl with a Monkey.* A final collection of stories about the character Nachman is to be published by Penguin Putnam. He died on May 10, 2003.

BHARATI MUKHERJEE is the author of six novels (*Desirable Daughters, Leave It to Me, The Holder of the World, Jasmine, Wife, The Tiger's Daughter*) and two collections of short stories (*The Middleman and Other Stories, Darkness*); she is also the co-author, with Clark Blaise, of two nonfiction books (*The Sorrow and the Terror, Days and Nights in Calcutta*). A member of the American Academy of Arts and Sciences, she has received a Guggenheim Fellowship, a Senior Canada Council Fellowship, and an NEA grant. She teaches at the University of California, Berkeley.

NICHOLAS PAPANDREOU's most recent novel, *Kleptomnemon,* imagines a world where people's memories are stolen, then traded on the marketplace. His forthcoming book, *Politics in the First Person,* analyzes the role of narrative and story-telling in the lives of famous Greek politicians. He works part-time at the Ministry of the Aegean with a team of dreamers who want to save the islands from the wrath of over-construction. Most of his published short stories, essays, magazine articles and book excerpts are available on his website: www.nikospapandreou.gr

LUC SANTE was born in Verviers, Belgium. He is the author of *Low Life, Evidence,* and *The Factory of Facts* and co-editor, with Melissa Holbrook Pierson, of *O.K. You Mugs: Writers on Movie Actors.* He is the recipient of a Whiting Writer's Award, a Guggenheim Fellowship, an Award in Literature from the American Academy of Arts and Letters, and a Grammy, for album notes, and is a Fellow of the American

Academy of Arts and Sciences. He is Visiting Professor of Writing and the History of Photography at Bard College, and he lives with his wife and son in Ulster County, New York.

GARY SHTEYNGART was born in Leningrad, USSR, in 1972, and came to the United States seven years later. His novel, *The Russian Debutante's Handbook*, won the Stephen Crane Award for First Fiction, was named a New York Times Notable Book, and was chosen as a best book of the year by the *Washington Post Book World* and *Entertainment Weekly*. His work has appeared in *The New Yorker, Granta, GQ,* the *New York Times,* and many other publications. He lives in New York City.

JOSEF ŠKVORECKÝ, who was born in 1924, is the author most recently of *When Eve Was Naked*. Among his earlier books are *The Cowards, The Bass Saxophone, The Engineer of Human Souls, The Bride of Texas,* and many others. He lives with his wife, Zdena, in Toronto, Ontario.

AMY TAN is the author of *The Joy Luck Club*, a beloved and internationally best-selling novel that explores the relationships of Chinese women and their Chinese-American daughters. She is also author of *The Kitchen God's Wife, The Hundred Secret Senses,* and two children's books. Her latest novel, *The Bonesetter's Daughter,* was published in 2001, and in the fall of 2003 she published a collection of nonfiction work entitled *The Opposite of Fate.*

NGUGI WA THIONG'O was born in Limuru, Kenya, in 1938, and was educated at Makerere University College in Kampala, Uganda. With eight novels, a book of short stories, a memoir, and five plays to his credit, Ngugi is one of the leading African writers and scholars at work today. His novels have been translated into more than thirty languages and have earned him a number of prizes, including the East African Novel Prize, the Paul Robeson Award for Artistic Excellence, Political Conscience and Integrity, and the Zora Neale Hurston–Paul Robeson

Award for artistic and scholarly achievement. He was recently named University of California Irvine's Distinguished Professor in the School of Humanities and director of the International Center for Writing and Translation, and in 2003 he was elected an honorary member in the American Academy of Arts and Letters.

"*Consistently engaging, sly, witty, understated (though still provocative) and written with simple elegance. . . . Like a powerful novel,* The Amateur *works in mysterious, subterranean ways.*"
—The New York Observer

THE AMATEUR

*An Independent Life of Letters*

In this unusual memoir of the life of the mind, the founding editor of *The Threepenny Review* reflects upon the choices she has made in pursuit of her vocation as a self-described "eighteenth-century man of letters." Wendy Lesser, one of our shrewdest cultural observers, describes how her education, her experiences, and the works of her favorite writers, artists, and performers have shaped and deepened her understanding of the world. She shows us how she has created an independent life as a writer, editor, and critic, free to follow her enthusiasms where they lead her. Whether her subject is Mark Morris's choreography, the delights of e-mail, the odd assortment of words that were born the same year she was, or the moral implications of giving to beggars (pondered by way of Charles Dickens and Henry James), Lesser's acute wisdom and elegant prose render a beguiling portrait of a remarkable mind at work.

Memoir/Essays/0-375-70381-0